Finding Hope in Times of Grief
is touching and strengthening...

"Grief is never invited. It shows up at the most unexpected times, and leaves us with a whirlwind of thoughts and emotions. Preston and Glenda Parrish have walked the road of grief and in their pain have found hope. I highly recommend this book to anyone who has had an encounter with grief."

GARY CHAPMAN, AUTHOR OF *THE FIVE LOVE LANGUAGES*

"Preston and Glenda Parrish have lived through what no parent ever wants to experience—the loss of a child. The key is how they have "lived through" grief that had the potential of paralyzing the progress of life. God intends for us to press on. He is the source of strength that points us forward through assurance that the Savior and Comforter the Lord Jesus Christ walks with us through every dark valley, teaching us how to look beyond our own grief so that we can reach out to others who may not know where to turn when their time of grief strikes. Delve into the richness of God's promises through their story of *Finding Hope in Times of Grief.*"

FRANKLIN GRAHAM, PRESIDENT & CEO BILLY GRAHAM
EVANGELISTIC ASSOCIATION, SAMARITAN'S PURSE

"Life presents unprecedented pain when experiencing the sudden death of someone precious. Preston and Glenda Parrish have learned this lesson firsthand in the untimely death of their son, Nathan. Because of God's faithfulness, they discovered that death ushers you to a front row seat of God's unending mercy and grace. I rejoiced reading their book and remembered vividly my own parallel experience of the darkest moments of despair and the hope found in the holy intimacy with God. He healed my broken heart and bound up my wounds after the sudden, tragic death of my astronaut husband. May you be encouraged and filled with hope as you read this wonderful book."

EVELYN HUSBAND THOMPSON, WIDOW OF COLUMBIA
SPACE SHUTTLE COMMANDER, RICK HUSBAND

"Are your thoughts over the loss of someone dear to you paralyzing you? Do you feel hopeless in facing the cold, hard reality of your loss? Preston and Glenda have personally found that HOPE in God's faithfulness in their tragic loss really does exist and can be known in the midst of deep grief. Their honesty, transparency, faith, and perseverance will bless, strengthen, encourage, and help you during your hard moments and difficult days."

JOSEPH NORTHCUT, DIRECTOR OF CHURCH MINISTRIES, GRIEFSHARE.ORG

"If you've ever sat at a graveside, heartbroken and lost, this is the book for you. With tender grace and deep authenticity, the Parrishes will walk with you through the rocky roads of grief. This book is a treasure of truth written by those who understand that dance between sorrow and hope."

LYSA TERKEURST, AUTHOR OF *WHAT HAPPENS WHEN WOMEN SAY YES TO GOD* AND *MADE TO CRAVE*

"I can think of several families right now that I want to hand this book to. Preston and Glenda have shared so openly and honestly about their own tragedy and grief. In a word, this book is REAL. Real with the pain we feel when we lose someone we love. And real with the hope we have in the God of comfort."

MATTHEW WEST, GRAMMY NOMINEE AND DOVE AWARD WINNER, SINGER AND SONGWRITER

FINDING HOPE
in TIMES *of* GRIEF

PRESTON *and* GLENDA
PARRISH

HARVEST HOUSE PUBLISHERS

EUGENE, OREGON

Cover by e210 Design, Eagan, Minnesota

Cover photo © Corbis Photography / Veer

FINDING HOPE IN TIMES OF GRIEF
Copyright © 2011 by Preston and Glenda Parrish
Published by Harvest House Publishers
Eugene, Oregon 97402
www.harvesthousepublishers.com

Library of Congress Cataloging-in-Publication Data
　Parrish, Preston
　Finding hope in times of grief / Preston and Glenda Parrish.
　　p. cm.
　Includes bibliographical references.
　ISBN 978-0-7369-3075-8 (pbk.)
　1. Consolation. 2. Children—Death—Religious aspects—Christianity. 3. Parrish, Nathan, 1980-
2006—Death and burial. 4. Parrish, Preston. 5. Parrish, Glenda. I. Parrish, Glenda. II. Title.
BV4907.P27 2011
248.8'66—dc22

2010015984

Printed in the United States of America

11 12 13 14 15 16 17 18 19 / VP-NI / 10 9 8 7 6 5 4 3 2 1

With gratitude to God for Nathan

Because he is Home safe,
we do not "grieve as do the rest who have no hope."
1 Thessalonians 4:13

ACKNOWLEDGMENTS

We want to express our deepest love for Hannah, Gregory, and JesseRuth, who have walked through grief and found hope together with us. Their prayers, understanding, patience, and support are gifts from our heavenly Father. They have their own stories to tell, which we'll let them do in their own way and time.

Contents

Preface

GRIEF IS not "pretty."

We don't like to think about it, and in our society—and even in the church—we go to great lengths to avoid it, or at least to dress it up as best we can.

Yet no matter how we try to insulate ourselves from it, it's impossible to get past the fact that none of us is immune to grief. When it does finally hit us and throw our lives into anguished upheaval, the pressing question becomes, how do we deal with it?

In the course of dealing with our own personal sorrow, we have walked through many hard moments and difficult days. Some of the time, our walk has been in full view of others, and we're sure their assessment of us has indeed been "not pretty." Guess what—often, what others have *not* seen has been even less pretty.

In one sense, it would have been easier just to leave things there: whatever people have seen and thought, they've seen and thought…whatever people haven't seen, so much the better. Doing so would have spared us from further scrutiny and analysis by people not struggling their way through grief. After all, who likes to embarrass themselves?

Then…the opportunity came to write this book. After weighing it prayerfully, we felt we should do it.

Why? It certainly wasn't to weary people with the details of our own personal story. We had plenty of other things we could do. We have, however, looked into too many weeping eyes and heard too many pained cries—some loud and wailing, some barely audible yet nonetheless impassioned—to just turn away and keep safely to ourselves about this experience of grief that will come to each of us at some time in our life.

While we've talked with quite a number of people about their personal grief, our sense is that many more need some of the insights that have come to us, not just from theory, but through facing cold, hard reality.

For such dear people, we felt we had to speak more fully about what—and ultimately, *whom*—we have encountered in our grief. So, in an effort to connect with our fellow travelers on this tough road, we have written this book.

One note of caution is that if, right now, you just don't want to think more about the "stuff" that goes with grief, you should stop reading. We understand. This book will be available when you do feel the need for it.

But if at this moment you're searching—perhaps desperately—for some shred of something that might help you through your own hard moments and difficult days, we've chosen in the pages that follow to be vulnerable, with the risk that accompanies vulnerability. Our prayer is that our openness about our own grief will be helpful to you.

If it is, then the risk will have been worth it.

May God comfort you in your grief.

Sustained by our risen Savior,
Preston and Glenda Parrish

This hope we have as an anchor of the soul,
a hope both sure and steadfast
and one which enters within the veil.

HEBREWS 6:19

A Confession

THE SCENE was surreal.

My mind flashed back almost 35 years to homeroom as a junior in high school. Several rows of desks over, I laid eyes on her for the first time. She wore a white denim jacket and carried her books in a backpack. Her long curly locks and deep dimples spoke volumes about her intriguing personality. Her name was Glenda, and she was no ordinary girl. In fact, just 34 months later, she would become my wife for life, our young but certain hearts drawn together by a deep desire to serve the Lord Jesus Christ in evangelism (not to mention she was irresistibly cute, with a warm and godly spirit).

Yet now, on this Southern winter day, the setting was very different.

We were standing by a grave…the grave of our 25-year-old son Nathan, who had unexpectedly died in a rock-climbing fall just one day after we buried my father who, other than Glenda, had been my closest friend.

I never imagined all those years ago that it would come to

this—the two of us grieving together not only over the passing of a beloved parent (which most of us expect) but also over the sudden death of a dear son whom God had given us. Yet the freshly turned earth and the not-yet-wilted flowers spoke the truth: my aged, ailing father and our young, fit son had both died. Nathan's funeral had taken place at an age we would all deem too early, and now the two of us, as well as our family, would have to deal with this new reality and go on…but how very hard it would be.

As a husband and father whose own heart was already torn and broken, I sought to be strong and faith-filled for Glenda and our other three children. Minutes after receiving the sheriff deputy's phone call informing us of Nathan's death, I prayed for God's help. And He did indeed help me—in notifying our two older children, Hannah and Gregory, and then our 11-year-old daughter, JesseRuth; in making Nathan's funeral arrangements; and in listening to, talking with, and holding Glenda through the long months that followed.

Although I was vulnerable with Glenda in our grief, my own worst moments of sobbing and crying out to God came when I was alone. "O God, O God, O God," I blurted out time and time again. "Help me, Father, help me…" Even then, however, I knew that the grief of the woman who physically bore Nathan—who felt him move within her before ever he saw the light of day, and who labored painfully and hard to bring him into this world—was at least as deep as my own.

Because of our decades-long walk with Christ, though, I knew also that our grief would become a frame around a picture of God's all-sufficient grace, grace that is great enough to infuse even our worst moments with hope. That experience of grace has indeed been ours, and it is what we share with you.

At this point, however, I really must make a two-part confession.

The first part is that "finding hope in times of grief" is not likely a subject that anyone would aspire to address. To do so—at least with credibility—requires not only having a personal and real experience of hope but also a personal and real experience of raw, unabated grief.

While that may sound simple enough, it brings me to the second part of my confession—namely, that while I thought I knew about grief, I really did not.

This discovery was somewhat surprising to me because Glenda and I have devoted our lives to proclaiming the gospel. We've served the Lord in the context of the local church, interacting in many situations of pastoral need. I've come face-to-face with horrid earthly tragedies while working in evangelical relief efforts across the globe. As a law enforcement chaplain, I've ministered to victims and next-of-kin in some of the most heartbreaking, gut-wrenching scenes imaginable. And like most people, we have certainly faced previous situations of death and near-death in our family that drove us to our knees.

I thought I knew...but as we walked away from the grave where Nathan's body now lay, I was finding out how limited my understanding of grief really was. In short, Glenda and I were now embarking on a journey that, while we did not choose it, would take us deeper than we had yet been, both in the trials of life and in our walk with Christ.

We are aware that others have suffered far more (and far better) than us, and that we still have much to learn, but it is out of this walk of grief and grace that we now write. Glenda's honesty and transparency, and her faith and perseverance, will especially bless, strengthen, encourage, and help you. It has done that for me.

Because you're reading this book, you may well have discovered, as we have, that life is fragile and fleeting. Moses reflected on this fact, saying:

> In the morning they are like grass which sprouts anew...
> Toward evening it fades and withers away (Psalm 90:
> 5-6).

You never know when you yourself are going to be immersed in a scene of sorrow that isn't merely a nightmare from which you can simply awake. In fact, you may be there right now—or know someone who is—through the death of a child, a sibling, a spouse, a parent, or someone else dear to you.

Thousands of American families are there right now because their loved ones in the military have heroically sacrificed their lives in the defense of liberty. Others are there because someone they loved lost perspective to the point where he or she took actions that ended their precious life. Many others are no doubt there just because they live in a world where people get sick and die, or pass away through unexpected events.

Whatever the cause of your grief, our prayer is for you to discover, as we have, the faithfulness of God, who sent His one and only Son, the Lord Jesus Christ, as "a man of sorrows and acquainted with grief" (Isaiah 53:3).

May you know the embrace of His everlasting arms (Deuteronomy 33:27) as you walk a step at a time, a moment at a time, a breath at a time, through deep waters of suffering.

May you find that the confidence of His resurrection victory over the grave is the unshakable foundation that gives you reason, and makes it possible, to go on with life.

In short, through the pages that follow, may "the God of all comfort" (2 Corinthians 1:3) become even more real to you personally, so much so that you too find hope in your time of grief.

From Glenda…Our Times

There is an appointed time for everything.
And there is a time for every event under heaven—
a time to give birth and a time to die.

ECCLESIASTES 3:1-2

I thought I would marry…and I did.

I thought I would give birth to children…and I did.

I thought I would love them and watch them grow…and I did.

I thought I would die before any of my children…*I did not.*

Nathan—I always loved his name. I never tired of saying it, even when the tone in which it was said may have meant he was in trouble.

Born November 17, 1980, Nathan, we quickly learned, was persistent, articulate, and funny. He was a gift from God to Preston and me, and we raised him to understand who God is and what faith in Christ means. As a result, Nathan came to faith early and always had keen spiritual insight and discernment about people.

He was not perfect, though, and struggled through adolescence before recommitting his life to the Lord in his early twenties. From that moment on, he grew in his faith and wanted everyone he encountered to know that Jesus loved him or her. He had an urgency that I've seldom seen about communicating this message—perhaps because he was so keenly aware of what life is like outside of a vibrant, personal walk with Christ.

One of my last memories of Nathan is of him telling a grocery store clerk, "Jesus loves you." When he left our house after Christmas 2005 to return to his job in California, I did not know it was the last time in this life that I would ever see him.

I will forever hear the words that came to us by phone a few short days later: "We have found a body." Nathan's lifeless corpse lay at the base of a rock wall in Southern California's San Jacinto Mountains. We learned that as he was climbing solo up the face of the peak known as Tahquitz, along a route called Open Book (he loved pushing himself to accomplish new challenges), the weather deteriorated, winds began to blow forcefully, and he fell several hundred feet, hitting the ground in the cleft between two rocks.

I don't remember much immediately after the phone call, but I do remember collapsing on our bathroom floor and screaming, "My child, my child, my child…Jesus, help me!"

In the hours and days that followed, I felt an intense sorrow about never again being able to tell Nathan I loved him. I went through his whole life repeatedly in my mind. I would laugh when I thought about funny things he would do or say, cry when I thought about how amazingly thoughtful and kind he always was, and then cry even more as I panicked over whether he really knew the tremendous respect and love everyone in our family had for him.

It was the most vulnerable time in my life. One minute I would feel great joy over all that we had watched him accomplish, and the next minute I would become weighed down by thoughts about how I could have been a better parent. Never have I ridden such a roller coaster.

I spent most of the day after Nathan died rocking back and forth in a glider chair in our bedroom. It was the same glider I had used to rock JesseRuth when she was an infant…feeding her, singing to her, praying over her. Now, just 11 years later, I was in it weeping over her dead brother. How unnatural, how strange!

In those moments, God spoke to me—inaudibly, internally, but in a voice that nonetheless ministered to the deepest needs of my heart.

"*Glenda,*" He said, "*Nathan is* MY *child.*"

That message hit me like a lightning bolt, and it was absolutely right. Preston and I had received Nathan as a gift from God. We had cherished that gift and the part we had to play in his short life, but that time and season were now over.

While grief gripped my insides, the wondrous truth that God Himself was Nathan's heavenly Father helped take me where I needed to be: closer to the Lord Jesus. I found Him to be the Source of comfort and strength.

In the days that followed, I continued to agonize over the loss of Nathan's presence with us. However, every time that I would go down the road of despair, God would meet me there by His Spirit— assuring me that Nathan was His child and that He would take care of him, even though I no longer could.

How thankful I was that I too am God's child, by His grace and as a result of faith in Christ. To be adrift in this sea of grief without that relationship and without His promise never to leave us or forsake us would be unthinkable.

Maybe, though, that's your situation at this moment. Maybe you have been blown into a storm of loss and pain you didn't see coming and never imagined possible. Maybe you're feeling as though waves are engulfing you and it's just a matter of minutes until you go under and never come back up. Maybe you feel as though you're a long way from knowing God.

Here is some good news: You cannot control the awful

circumstances that have befallen you, but you can choose to face them and go through them as God's child.

The Bible says, "Everyone who calls on the name of the Lord shall be saved" (Acts 2:21).

It also says, "Behold, now is the day of salvation" (2 Corinthians 6:2).

Jesus told the religious leader Nicodemus, "You must be born again" (John 3:7).

If you have received Jesus into your heart by faith and asked Him to forgive your sins, you *are* His child. God's Word promised: "As many as received Him, to them He gave the right to become children of God, even to those who believe in His name" (John 1:12). If you haven't yet made this choice, then this moment—of all moments—is the time to do so. Just call out to God with a prayer (prayer is simply talking with God) something like this:

> *Dear Lord Jesus, thank You that You love me. I realize that I have sinned and need Your forgiveness and salvation. I believe that You died on the cross for my sins and rose from the grave. I want to turn from my sins and follow You. Please forgive me for my sins and make me Your child. By faith, I receive You into my heart as my Lord and Savior. Help me to live for You, now and always. Thank You for hearing and answering my prayer.*

When you do this, you become the child of a perfect Father who, through Christ, has entered into our weakness and vulnerability.

You become the child of the One who numbers all our days, and who alone knows the day we will be born and the day we will die.

You become the child of the One who has written every one of our days in His book, even before there was one.

You become the child of the One who promises the strength we need for every day.

You become the child of the One who will be faithful to carry you through the paths before you, which look so foreboding.

In the midst of the storm, God will give you rest and strength. He will do all this because you cling to His Son, the Lord Jesus Christ.

Jesus Himself said, "Come to Me…and you will find rest for your souls" (Matthew 11: 28-29).

As His child, you will be able to say with the psalmist, "My times are in Your hand" (Psalm 31:15).

In His hand, even this dark, dark hour won't be the final season in your life. God Himself will give you

> A garland instead of ashes,
> The oil of gladness instead of mourning,
> The mantle of praise instead of a spirit of
>   fainting (Isaiah 61:3).

PART 1

The Call: Hope

So…
     The funeral is over…
The people who temporarily turned aside to grieve with you and to honor your deceased loved one—or loved ones—have now returned to their own busy lives…

The flowers have faded, and perhaps pots of dried-up stems and leaves sit beside your trash can…

The meal deliveries from caring friends have stopped…

The phone doesn't ring quite so much anymore…

The cards don't fill the mailbox the way they once did, either—just the usual bills and junk mail, and maybe, painfully, a piece of mail now and then addressed to the one whose absence saps your strength virtually every moment of every day…

And no matter how you feel about it, morning still comes and night still falls, over and over and over again, with everyone and everything around you saying, "You just have to go on" while everything within you undeniably groans, "*But nothing is the same.*"

What are you supposed to do with this load of experience and emotion that has landed on you and now weighs on every aspect of your being?

Are you just supposed to "get over it"?

Are you just supposed to "move on"?

Are you just supposed to resign yourself to the idea, expressed in the words of the Bible's book of Job:

> Man is born for trouble,
> As sparks fly upward (Job 5:7).

Is the order of the day simply to put on your best stoical face and avoid letting what is going on in your heart and mind break through and make others uncomfortable, while inside you grope to somehow find comfort, meaning, and strength?

Are you now destined to live the rest of your days as if caught in some swirling amusement park ride from which you cannot exit and that, in fact, makes you feel rather sick?

Is that it?

Or…might there be—maybe…just maybe…somehow…some way—something out there called *hope* that you can find and cling to like a sure and steady anchor in a churning sea?

Is there some balm that is sufficient to soothe your weary, aching soul in this present painful moment, and to give you renewed anticipation of experiencing not just tragedy but blessing in the days to come?

Simply put, can you ever begin to feel better and to see this event that has befallen you assume a place of purpose and value in your life and in the lives of others?

The answer, according to God's Word, the Bible, is a resounding *yes*.

The writer of the New Testament book of Hebrews made this declaration:

> This hope we have as an anchor of the soul,
> a hope both sure and steadfast
> and one which enters within the veil
> (Hebrews 6:19).

As uncertain as you may be right now about what these words mean and whether they can apply to you, we have personally found that hope really does exist and that it really can be known, even in the midst of grief.

In fact, far from being a rarity, an exceptional experience that only a few special people are meant to find, it is in reality a calling—*your* calling—offered and extended to you by the hand of God Himself.

In the Bible's New Testament, the apostle Paul prayed: "I pray that the eyes of your heart may be enlightened, so that you will know what is the hope of His calling" (Ephesians 1:18).

Do you want to know more about what this biblical hope is… about what it does…and about why it does it?

Read on…and as you do, know that God Himself is reaching out to you to draw you close in His tender, loving embrace.

1

Hope: What It Is

THROUGH HIS OWN HARD TIMES, our son Nathan came to have hope.

For us as his parents, his death drove us also to a deeper experience of biblical hope than we had ever known before.

Often, it's only when the Lord Jesus Christ is the only One to whom we can cling that we realize He really is all we need.

That was Nathan's story.

Born with extraordinary spiritual sensitivity and trained up "in the way he should go" (Proverbs 22:6), Nathan was nonetheless lured for a while into a parched land of pleasures that pass.[1] The particular snares into which he stepped don't matter so much here—all of us are vulnerable to temptations.

What matters is that, as a teen reared to walk with Christ, he somehow became absorbed with a crowd of peers who had other aims, and he chose to wander with them into a spiritual wilderness. We certainly were not perfect parents; only God Himself is the perfect Father. However, as Nathan learned, while we all must make our choices in life, we can't choose our consequences. They come built-in with our choices. Choices—whether for good or for ill—set in motion a chain of effects that we can attempt to manage but cannot truly control.

During Nathan's wandering years, we prayed and, as it were, peered through the window many days (and many long nights) to catch a glimpse of him returning home. At times, we despaired that we might never see his familiar figure coming over the horizon toward us, or more accurately, toward the One we serve.

Yet the Lord Jesus Christ eventually had the last word in Nathan's life. Like the prodigal son of old (Luke 15:11-24), Nathan finally came to his senses and returned to his heavenly Father. He repented of his sins and came to walk with Christ, especially during what were ultimately the last two years of his life on earth.

Yet, like the Old Testament patriarch Jacob, who limped after his wrestling match with God (Genesis 32:24-32), Nathan also "limped." Nathan's limp was not in his gait—it was in some of his reasoning and social interaction, which were impacted by the dissipation of his adolescent years.

Even as he went on to accomplish some significant milestones in his life—including college graduation and work as a camp instructor—Nathan himself knew that he limped in these areas, and it frustrated him. He had great regret over the challenges in his life that were the result of his choices. He so wished that it had not come to be this way…but it had. Even though Christ had made him a new person, Nathan still bore some "grave wrappings"—like Lazarus, whom Christ raised from the dead and called forth from the tomb (John 11:44).

Nathan's response was to look to God in His Word for some truth that he could cling to, that would give him hope. He found it in the Old Testament book of Lamentations (a title derived from a Latin word meaning "to cry aloud"). There, Jeremiah the prophet wrote:

> I remember my affliction and my wandering,
>   the bitterness and the gall.
> I well remember them,
>   and my soul is downcast within me.
> Yet this I call to mind
>   and therefore I have hope:
>
> Because of the LORD's great love we are not consumed,
>   for his compassions never fail.
> They are new every morning;
>   great is your faithfulness.
> I say to myself, "The LORD is my portion;
>   therefore I will wait for him."
>
> The LORD is good to those whose hope is in him,
>   to the one who seeks him;
> it is good to wait quietly
>   for the salvation of the LORD.
> It is good for a man to bear the yoke
> while he is young (Lamentations 3:19-27 NIV).

This portion of Scripture was one Nathan's favorites. The hope it speaks of meant so much to him that he kept in his wallet a small scrap of paper on which he had printed it in his distinctive, left-handed scrawl. It was something that he read repeatedly, that infused him with hope, and that helped him keep going in his walk with the Lord despite the challenges he faced.

That scrap of paper was with him the day he fell. The hope of

Christ carried him through life, and escorted him through death into its fulfillment in heaven.

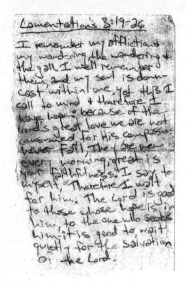

As Glenda and I began to pick up the pieces following Nathan's departure, we found ourselves in the same position—clinging for dear life to the hope of Christ day by day and anticipating its fulfillment for us as well when God's purposes for our days here are completed.

So, what is this hope that sustains us and that God offers to you as well?

First, let's clarify what hope is not.

Hope is not wishful thinking, or whatever pleasant illusion we may manufacture.

It isn't some fantasy on which we fixate, in order to mystically influence events or, at least, to make ourselves feel better.

Some time ago in an airport, I observed such an effort at a shoeshine stand located next to a lottery ticket dispenser. The attendant took advantage of a lull in business to step next door and purchase a ticket. Returning to his stand, he took a seat in the chair. Next, he closed his eyes and lifted his hands heavenward, clutching his lottery ticket. Hesitating for a moment, he appeared to whisper a quick prayer under his breath. Finally, he lowered his arms, opened the ticket, looked at it, and then…he tossed it in the trash and returned to shining shoes!

As laughable (or pitiful) as this scene was, it gives us a picture of how a lot of people view hope—as something you wish for, perhaps against all odds, perhaps with a token flourish of religion, that's so farfetched it probably won't happen in a million years.

Eighteenth-century British writer Samuel Johnson said, "There are multitudes whose life is nothing but a continuous lottery; who are always within a few months of plenty and happiness."[2]

That is not biblical hope.

True biblical hope is a settled confidence based on objective fact and enduring truth. It depends not on ritual or chance, but is founded in the God of salvation, who in Christ has shown Himself to be full of lovingkindness, compassion, and faithfulness.

True hope does not give in to despair. Rather, because of who God is, it patiently waits and confidently expects good from God— here and now, and for eternity—regardless of the severity of one's personal storms.

God-based hope goes hand in hand with joy because it depends on the constancy of the One who holds us in His hand rather than on our own fickle emotions.

That's what Jeremiah was saying in that passage that was so precious to Nathan, and it's what we can personally possess, all because of the Lord Jesus Christ, "who is our hope" (1 Timothy 1:1).

It comes down to this: God so loved the world that He sent His one and only Son, Jesus—

> who came not just as a spirit but also as flesh like us…
> who came as a Man of sorrows, acquainted with grief…
> who was tempted like us yet did not sin…
> who suffered for our sins even unto death…
> who conquered the grave on the third day…

who returned to His Father's right hand in heaven
where He intercedes for us now…
who will receive all who have trusted in Him for
    salvation into heaven upon their death…
and who will one day return and make all things new…

These objective facts and enduring truths are the basis upon which we can embrace and draw strength from the promise that God Himself spoke to His people through the prophet Jeremiah: "'For I know the plans that I have for you,' declares the LORD, 'plans for welfare and not for calamity to give you a future and a hope'" (Jeremiah 29:11).

In other words, we can count on the risen, living Christ to make blessing and not grief the ultimate summation of our lives. That's better than anything this world can offer—including a lottery ticket.

From Glenda…Our Times

A time to mourn and a time to dance…
ECCLESIASTES 3:4

The rain is pounding hard on the tin roof. As I sit here, I hear nothing but it…and my thoughts.

The thoughts never stop coming, and often they become louder than any words and everything else around. They are constant and unending—old thoughts, new thoughts, good thoughts, and bad thoughts. Somewhere in all of them, however, is Nathan.

During the days immediately following Nathan's burial, my mind was filled with a rapid, anxious stream of thoughts about him:

> Did he know how much I loved him?
> I will never see him play soccer again.
> I won't ever be able to see him marry.
> Did he experience fear or pain as he fell?
> I will never know his children.
> What did he see as he entered heaven?
> I will never hear him say, "What's up?" again.
> He loved to dance—did he break out in the biggest
>   jig ever when he got to heaven?
> At what moment exactly did he fall from that
>   mountain face?

The thoughts went on and on, and none of my questions ever seemed to be followed with a concrete answer.

When our entire family gathers, we are reminded that someone is missing from our family equation. It doesn't matter what we do or what anyone says—nothing can fill the empty place at our table.

Preston, Hannah, Gregory, and JesseRuth all miss him in ways unique to their relationship with Nathan as a son or brother. Our son-in-law, Max, who knew Nathan in his final years here, recalls him from his own viewpoint.

For our daughter-in-law, Becca, and for our grandchildren— AnnaPreston and her younger siblings, brother Adsem and his twin sister Alsey Bea—missing Nathan will be a learned part of their life's landscape, since they all came into our lives after Nathan's death. It seems like it would have been fitting for them too to have known and been enriched by him.

In prayer one morning, I was telling the Lord about my deep

despair over all the things I continually thought about Nathan. This Scripture came to mind:

> I would have despaired unless I had believed that I would see the goodness of the LORD in the land of the living (Psalm 27:13).

I immediately recognized that my despair was going to have to transport my mind to God instead of keeping me weighed down in my loss. The Holy Spirit spoke to my heart and made it clear to me that I was going to have to turn my thoughts toward all the ways God had previously brought me through difficult circumstances and trust that He would be faithful to stay with me and walk me through this valley of grief.

Sometime after I planted this verse in my heart, I looked up the meaning of the word "despair." Despair means "to lose, give up, or be without hope. It speaks of complete despondency.

Bingo! That is exactly how I felt before turning to God with my grief. Moments of reflecting on Nathan's life were so torturous that I sometimes just wanted to lie in my bed. While I delighted in his memory, missing him so terribly sometimes made me feel that I couldn't breathe.

Once I was able to place my despair—or lack of hope—at the feet of Jesus, hope arose in me because of my relationship and experience with Him. I found confidence that He would be with me as I walked through these days.

I have to be honest and say that it is not always easy to direct my thoughts toward God. But when I do, I gain new strength and I am able to keep moving forward.

Psalm 27:13 has become my theme verse during this season of my life. As you walk through your own personal days of grief, it is important that you too have specific portions of God's Word to which you can hold.

Recently I spoke to a woman whose young granddaughter had just died unexpectedly and tragically. For the most part, I simply listened to her, because I've learned that others' words to those who are grieving are sometimes just an attempt to fill an awkward silence and don't really connect with the aching heart. I did share with her, however, that this verse is the theme of my life right now and encouraged her to consider it for herself.

My days would be full of despair if I did not know a God who had met me at every turn in the road. It is He whom I can trust to get me through the rest of this life, no matter what comes into my path. Here are just a few of the things He has done that I remember:

- My life changed from one of aimlessness to one of purpose and joy when I asked Jesus into my heart as a teen.

- He brought a boy into my high school homeroom whom I loved almost immediately and who later became my husband.

- One day He called that boy, to whom I have now been married for decades, to full-time vocational ministry.

- He was faithful when we spent a summer as short-term missionaries, ministering to Americans in Mexican jails on drug charges, while I was pregnant with our firstborn.

- He safely brought our four children into this world.

- He strengthened and helped them when they were sick and scared.

- He healed our older son, Gregory, after he suffered a severe head injury in a skateboard accident.

- He protected Nathan in a potentially fatal car accident before he returned to the Lord.

- He has brought me through all these moments and days since I learned of Nathan's death.

Make your own list of God's faithfulness to you—I promise it will encourage you when you need it!

Perhaps you are sitting in a seat of despair right now, and your own thoughts over the loss of someone dear to you are paralyzing you. If so, you really can have hope. The ache we each feel will likely never go away this side of heaven, but God wants to move us beyond despair. He wants us to remember the ways He has been faithful to us. He wants us, through all the days that remain for us, to live a life full of His love.

The biggest reason not to despair is found in the truth that He desires to receive us into heaven, where we will live for eternity in His presence and be with all those we have loved here who also have trusted Him. There the time will indeed have come to dance together around His throne.

2

———❧❧———

An Anchor Sure and Steadfast: What Hope Does

H AVE YOU EVER BEEN in a storm at sea?
     I'm thinking of the kind of storm that is an event to re-
member, not just a brief bout of wind and rain that stirs up a few
whitecaps—a storm that immerses you in forces of nature that are
ferocious and that seem capable of tearing apart everything surrounding you and of swallowing you whole.

I've been in a few situations approaching that description. Over
the years, I've spent a number of days and nights on boats and ships.
I've sailed in the Caribbean…the North Atlantic…the Mediterranean, as well as on lakes and rivers, in vessels ranging from luxury
liners to ferries and fishing boats.

Generally, I've enjoyed these voyages—except, that is, for a few
stormy ones. Those exceptions left me longing for land, or at least
for a position of stability in the midst of a churning sea. Sometimes,
though, the only way I could find "comfort" was by lying strapped
in a bunk so as not to be tossed about on the crest of an angry swell,

37

and by trying to ignore the internal heaving that was taking place among most of the other passengers and that was threatening me as well. (Great fun, huh?)

Even on family outings, we've had a few adrenaline-producing moments. One summer afternoon Glenda, Hannah, JesseRuth, and I were lazily drifting on a lake in a sailboat. Since there was very little breeze, I hadn't bothered to lower the sail or drop an anchor in order to hold our position. Glenda was reclining on deck with her eyes closed; Hannah and JesseRuth were painting their nails. As the captain, I was savoring this occasion of being in command—of the sailboat, of my "crew," of the lake…in short, of all of life. What an idiot!

Without notice, a phantom wind streaked across the lake, filling our limp sail, jerking the line for controlling the boom out of my hand, and spinning the sail around on its mast, madly driving us across the lake, completely out of control. So much for my command of things!

Momentarily stunned, I managed to regroup and work my way along the deck to the end of the boom line in an effort to restore my control of the sail. However, not being the most experienced sailor, I overreacted when I grabbed it, pulling it too tight and intensifying the force of the unrelenting wind. Now we were moving at an even greater speed while also being tipped dangerously sideways, with the port side of the deck actually in the water and the starboard side jutting high up into the sky like a mountain waiting to be climbed.

As I fought to restore order to the situation, I saw out of the corner of my eye that JesseRuth—only about eight years old at the time—was extending herself as far as she could over that skyward-pointing rail in an effort to avoid sliding down the angled deck into the water. I became afraid that she was going to go overboard or that the boat might capsize on top of her, and us.

Then, in the midst of all these developments, thunder suddenly boomed from the sky. Bolts of lightning began shooting toward us from the ominous clouds that had massed overhead. Dartlike drops of rain began pelting us.

At this point, one of our family's favorite fictional characters, Winnie the Pooh—prone to getting himself into awkward situations—would have said, "Oh bother."

Well, to shorten the story, we were finally able to drop the sail, regain control of the boat, and use its small motor to work our way across the lake back to the marina. The only injuries were to my pride and reputation as a boat captain (I don't think my "crew" will ever entrust themselves to me on the water again!). Seldom have I been so glad to make it safely to solid ground…and I certainly developed a new appreciation for the importance of an anchor.

Tragedy and grief envelop us in a similar swirl for survival. Hope in Christ is the only thing that can steady and stabilize us, and enable us to survive life's storms until we reach safe harbor. As the writer to the Hebrews said: "This hope we have as an anchor of the soul, a hope both sure and steadfast" (Hebrews 6:19).

When this verse was written in the first century, anchors were standard equipment on ships sailing the Mediterranean. Sailors knew well their importance—their lives depended upon them. When fierce storms arose, the heavy iron hooks could grip rocks deep below the surface and, holding firmly to them, keep the storm-tossed ship from capsizing. The ride wouldn't be pleasant, but at least the crew could survive.

This function of the anchor made it a symbol of hope, especially for early Christians who could see similarities between the shape of an anchor and the cross. Even some ancient Roman coins utilized the image of the anchor to depict hope.

The apostle Paul, who was no stranger to stormy seas, knew the benefit of an anchor. The New Testament book of Acts, chapter 27, narrates his voyage from the port of Caesarea to imperial Rome. Under arrest and facing legal charges stirred up by Jewish leaders angered by his proclamation of the hope of the gospel, Paul had appealed his case to Caesar, which was his right as a Roman citizen. En route, a fierce and prolonged storm engulfed the ship on which he was being transported: "Neither sun nor stars appeared for many days, and no small storm was assailing us, from then on all hope of our being saved was gradually being abandoned" (Acts 27:20).

However, with prayer and encouragement from Paul, the crew persevered: "When the fourteenth night had come...about midnight the sailors began to surmise that they were approaching some land... Fearing that we might run aground somewhere on the rocks, they cast four anchors from the stern and wished for daybreak" (Acts 27:27, 29).

The chapter goes on to describe how God wonderfully preserved Paul and the crew. Maybe right now, though, you're feeling just like those sailors, all hope gradually being abandoned and wishing for daybreak. Maybe you've thrown at your situation every anchor you have at your disposal, but the winds are still howling, the sea is still churning, and you're just not sure you're going to survive.

If so, then the message for you at this very moment, in the depths of your grief, is this: *In Christ, God is offering you a hope that is firmly anchored to the solid rock of His own character and that will steady and stabilize you and see you through this storm, unimaginable as that outcome might presently be.*

This hope is not a mirage. It isn't something we must conjure up. It is an anchor that, rather than just bouncing along on life's bottom with no steadying, stabilizing effect, is steadfastly "hooked" onto God Himself and does not slip. It is a gift from God that we receive by faith and that is rooted in the accomplished fact of Christ's victory over death, when God raised Him on the third day after He died on the cross for our sins (more about that in chapter 6). It anticipates and will find its ultimate fulfillment in His promised return to establish His kingdom.

Meanwhile, between that accomplished past and promised future, in your own difficult here-and-now, the promise in the words of the prophet Isaiah is for you: "He will be the stability of your times, a wealth of salvation" (Isaiah 33:6).

In fact, He is the "captain" of our salvation, who is perfectly able to take us through the storm until we are safely home.

From Glenda…Our Times

A time to plant and a time to uproot what is planted…
ECCLESIASTES 3:2

As I write this, I'm at the beach.

This morning as I stood in the surf, waves crashed around me. I planted my feet in the sand.

The tidal currents agitated back and forth, and the sand began to shift beneath me.

The constant change in the tide made it harder and harder to maintain my balance. The question that arose in my mind was, *Will I be able to stand?*

This is also the exact question that Nathan's death immediately posed for me. As I said through tears to my dear friend Jodie when I first saw her, "What am I going to do?" In the hours, days, weeks, and months since Nathan died, I've seen that the answer depends on what I'm standing on—on where I plant my feet.

When a child is born, he or she is implanted in your heart. When someone you so dearly love dies, it feels like something has been uprooted in your heart, and it hurts. It's as if the ground you are standing on undergoes a seismic shift. Suddenly, you feel more vulnerable than ever before. Even if you previously thought you understood death, you may quickly learn that you know very little about it. Each moment becomes a challenge to survive and to have any confidence for the future rather than succumbing to grief-filled hopelessness.

If God had asked me the question, "Glenda, can I take Nathan from this earth now?" in all honesty I probably would have said, "No!" After all, I loved my son, and in my mind I was planning on watching him flourish in the talents and gifts that God had uniquely given him and planning on seeing his children.

However, God did not ask me. Nathan's death came upon our family as quickly as the storm came upon us that day we were in the sailboat on the lake. Even now, some hard days come upon me in much the same manner. Sometimes they come for a particular reason—a date, a destination, a conversation—but other days they come for no specific reason, and I find myself struggling to stand with any kind of stability.

I have learned I have to lean upon God more than ever to help me function when my heart is just plain broken. I have to plant my feet on the solid rock of God's promises in order not to topple over in grief's waves.

Nathan has now been in heaven for several years (from the perspective of earthly time). I have lived through enough stormy moments and days to know that they eventually pass. In the beginning, living through them seemed like being in a dream in which everything happens in slow motion and, no matter how hard you strain, you cannot get the experience to speed up and go faster. Even now, standing firm while going through them is sometimes difficult.

To make it through them, I now recognize I have to do two things. First, I ask God to hold me up so that I do not fall. I rely on His promise spoken through the prophet Isaiah: "I am the LORD your God, who upholds your right hand" (Isaiah 41:13).

When I ask God to hold me up and keep me from being overwhelmed by sorrow, He is always faithful to do so. Sometimes I sense His presence in an almost tangible way that enables me to raise my head and keep moving forward. Many times, I receive strength just from quietly reading my Bible. On occasion, His help comes to me through a friend who's there at just the right moment.

Recently, I wrote a friend who has stuck with me through all these days. I thanked her and her husband for helping me stand when I wasn't sure I could. Other people have come to us as well, reminding us of the truth that God hears our cries, sees every tear, and wants to hold us in His arms and comfort us.

Two days after Nathan died, God sovereignly orchestrated an entire day of very personalized ministry to us. Friends we have had throughout our ministry came one by one over a period of a few hours, heard our cries, and prayed with us.

All in all, it was as if the Lord Himself delivered a specially tailored "grief retreat" right to our door, and even into my bedroom. While I didn't have the stamina to see all who came as I sat in my trusty glider, I am deeply grateful for the love of our extended family and friends.

That day, God heard the prayers of His people and provided me with the comfort that comes from the Holy Spirit. Through those visits, He gave us the strength we would need for the days ahead.

God will hold you up too if you call out to Him. I can't tell you exactly how—He may well work in your heart and life differently than in mine. However, in my experience, there is no adequate place to take your broken heart but to Him. He alone is able to truly steady you and enable you to stand in your season of sorrow.

The second thing I do to make it through trying moments is to stand firm in the knowledge that God will hold me. I have known Him to do it before and can depend on Him to do it again. The Bible says:

> I waited patiently for the Lord;
> And He inclined to me, and heard my cry.
> He brought me up out of the pit of destruction,
>   out of the miry clay;
> And He set my feet upon a rock making my
>   footsteps firm (Psalm 40:1-2).

Time and time again through the years that I've walked with the Lord, I've cried out to Him for help, many times not even knowing exactly what to pray.

Time and time again over the years that I've walked with the Lord, He has responded by hearing and helping me, and by placing my feet on solid ground.

Today the ground under your feet may be rocked by tremors, but you *can* stand firm. If you fix your eyes on Christ, He will hold you up. Our hope can be safely placed in Him.

I have this confidence because, as the Bible says, "Tribulation brings about perseverance; and perseverance, proven character; and proven character, hope; and hope does not disappoint, because the love of God has been poured out within our hearts through the Holy Spirit who was given to us" (Romans 5:3-5).

At this very moment, may the hope and love that comes from God alone fill your heart.

3

Within the Veil: Why Hope
Does What It Does

THE MOMENT THE CURTAIN OPENED, their hearts—and their hope—sank.

I'm referring to Dorothy, Scarecrow, Tin Man, and Cowardly Lion, those beloved characters from *The Wizard of Oz*, which is perhaps the most-watched film in history. Probably you've seen it and recall how this particular scene happened.

In the film, which was based on the book by the same title, Dorothy finds herself suddenly transported to the mysterious Land of Oz after a tornado hits her home in her native Kansas. Accompanied by her dog Toto, Dorothy discovers Oz to be delightful but also terrifying. The sights and creatures she encounters captivate her—especially Scarecrow, who has no brain; Tin Man, who has no heart; and Cowardly Lion, who has no courage. Her real desire, though, is to return home.

Good Witch Glinda (no relation to my wife!) directs her to seek help from the Wizard of Oz who dwells in the Emerald City, which is reachable by following the yellow brick road. Clad in those now-famous magical ruby slippers, Dorothy, along with Toto and her three new friends, go "off to see the Wizard, the wonderful Wizard of Oz," in order to obtain what they each need.

On the way, they have to deal with constant threats from the Wicked Witch of the West. However, they make it safely to the Emerald City, where they have an audience with the great Wizard.

The Wizard appears before them as a larger-than-life head emerging from a giant, steaming cauldron. Speaking to them with a thunderous voice, he promises to grant their wishes in exchange for the Wicked Witch's broomstick. So, off they go to the Witch's castle.

Through a series of suspense-filled incidents, they wind up in possession of the Witch's broomstick and return to the Emerald City. Holding what they believe to be the ticket to their respective dreams, they are filled with anticipation as they once again appear before the Wizard.

Their dreams, however, are dashed when Toto wanders over to a small booth and pulls back a curtain, behind which Dorothy and her three friends see a small man using a control panel to create the projected image of power and greatness in which they had placed their hope. At least temporarily (everything works out fine in the end, of course), despair grips Dorothy, Scarecrow, Tin Man, and Cowardly Lion.

Part of the film's appeal is that every viewer identifies with that heart-sinking moment of bitter disappointment. In the midst of your own grief, you may well be feeling that way right now. Given what has befallen you, you may be thinking that whatever confidence you had about life here and now, and for the future, has evaporated. If so, you're not the first, and you're not alone.

In the Bible's Old Testament, a righteous man named Job lost his wealth, his *ten* children (I can't imagine such pain), and his health, and was reduced to such sorrow that "even his wife said to him, 'Do you still hold fast your integrity? Curse God and die!'" (Job 2:9).

Job, however, remained steadfast, even while covered with boils and sitting in a heap of ashes. But he was human, and in the course of his desperation cried, "Oh that I knew where I might find Him, that I might come to His seat!" (Job 23:3).

Perhaps that is your cry at this very moment. If so, it's crucial for you to know that, unlike the experience of Dorothy and her companions with the Wizard, hope in Christ is not a projected illusion or an empty figment of our imagination.

To the contrary, our hope is based on the fact that, in Christ, God has taken the initiative to come and find us, and that now— at this instant—Christ Himself is interceding for us. In Him our hope, and our sorrow, reside in the very presence of Almighty God.

To understand more about why this is so, it's helpful to consider how Jewish worship in the Old Testament pictured the hope found in Christ.

Some 1500 years before Christ appeared, the nation of Israel was suffering in Egypt under Pharaoh. God heard their cries and, through Moses, delivered them from bondage in Egypt, bringing them out to lead them to Canaan, the land He had promised them. En route, they came to Mount Sinai.

"Now Mount Sinai was all in smoke because the LORD descended upon it in fire; and its smoke ascended like the smoke of a furnace, and the whole mountain quaked violently...The LORD came down on Mount Sinai" (Exodus 19:18,20).

Calling Moses to the top of the mountain, the Lord proceeded to give him the Ten Commandments, as well as instructions for Israel's conduct and worship. Those instructions included a very specific pattern for a "sanctuary" (literally, a holy place), also called the tabernacle. Israel was a pilgrim nation at this time, and the tabernacle's design—which included moveable curtains and furnishings—made this structure transportable for the journey that lay ahead.

The focal point of the tabernacle was the Holy of Holies, an area where God instructed that the ark containing the stone tablets bearing the Ten Commandments be placed. On top of the ark were the mercy seat and the likenesses of two cherubim with outstretched wings made of a single piece of pure gold.

"There," said the Lord, "I will meet with you; and from above the mercy seat, from between the two cherubim which are upon the ark of the testimony, I will speak to you" (Exodus 25:22).

However, the Lord commanded that the Holy of Holies be separated from view and access by "a veil of blue and purple and scarlet material and fine twisted linen" (Exodus 26:31).

In other words, God's presence was not to be treated casually. Only the high priest—initially, Moses' brother, Aaron—could enter the Holy of Holies. He could do so only after meticulous preparations, and only one time a year—on the Day of Atonement—in order to present a blood sacrifice for Israel's sins.

Even after Israel had dwelt for some 500 years in Canaan and King Solomon had built the majestic temple in Jerusalem, the Holy of Holies remained the most important place, and it was still separated by a thick veil.

Over the remaining centuries until Christ appeared, even when the temple was plundered and rebuilt, it still had as its focal point the Holy of Holies, shielded by a veil. Ordinary people were not permitted to enter. Only the high priest could do so on their behalf. But when Christ shed His blood, breathed His last breath, and gave His life on the cross for our sins, all this changed.

On that day, Scripture records that "the veil of the temple was torn in two from top to bottom" (Matthew 27:51). This rending of the veil (which historians cite as being four inches thick) was something God Himself did in response to the blood shed by His sinless, spotless Son—"the Lamb of God who takes away the sin of the world!" (John 1:29).

Now, through Christ, God was inviting everyone into His presence. Whoever places their trust in Him may come. In the words of the New Testament writer to the Hebrews: "Therefore, brethren... we have confidence to enter the holy place by the blood of Jesus, by a new and living way which He inaugurated for us through the veil" (Hebrews 10:19-20).

Access into God's presence still isn't something for us to treat casually—it is, however, a privilege that God invites us to exercise continuously and freely, even boldly. "Therefore let us draw near with confidence to the throne of grace, so that we may receive mercy and find grace to help in time of need" (Hebrews 4:16).

The hope we have in Christ is far different from hoping in a small man hidden behind a curtain, merely projecting an image of power and greatness. Rather, it is confidence in the one Man in all of history who was qualified to deal with sin and to tear down the curtain separating us from God. The place where our hope takes hold is in the very presence of God, where all who trust in Christ will have their home and dwell forever.

Over the years, I've had the opportunity to travel many places, and I suppose there may be a few more I'd still like to see. Yet, more than ever since Nathan's death, heaven is the place I really look forward to going.

In the words of Dorothy, as she closed her eyes and clicked her heels together at the end of the film, "There's no place like home."

From Glenda...Our Times

A time to tear apart...
ECCLESIASTES 3:7

Why did my child die?

Why did my spouse die?

Why does everything around me seem to be dying?

Why do good people suffer?

Why did God not hear my prayers?

Maybe you are asking some of these questions right now...or maybe you're paralyzed and aren't able to ask any questions at all.

Or maybe the thought of asking God *why* makes you afraid.

You don't have to be very far into grief before the why question arises. Sometimes it rises up in your mind like a monster from some swamp; sometimes, other people raise it. One way or another it comes up and refuses to be buried along with your loved one.

Some say, "Faith never asks why." A wise woman once told me, "Faith often asks why and gets some interesting answers."

Ultimately, though, walking with Christ in a world that's out of order does sometimes mean that the why question calls for reliance upon God rather than leading to immediate resolution. God can be trusted with our questions, and He hears when we utter them to Him, whether in a scream or in a whisper.

My personal question was not so much, "Why did Nathan die?" but rather, "Why is grief so hard?" After all, Nathan loved the Lord...I love the Lord...heaven is home for both of us...why did his death hurt so much, and why was continuing on here without him so difficult?

The first year after Nathan died, I found it hard to do many of the usual things I had done before. I had little interest in casual chit-chat and mundane activities because weightier matters loomed before me. The fact is that an explosion took place in our family the minute we heard the news of Nathan's fatality. It forced upon me personal questions that took precedence in my mind:

- Nathan asked me so many times to sit down and have tea with him. Sometimes I did; other times I thought I was too busy. Why didn't I drop everything for a few precious minutes every time he asked?

- He had crocheted a toboggan for me for Christmas. Why didn't I express my appreciation more?

- If I had known the morning he left our home after Christmas that I would never see him again on this earth, I would have more deeply savored those last minutes together. Why didn't I?

I still don't have answers to some of my questions, but I do know that I have had to take the questions that have come into my mind and place them at the feet of Jesus. I have to say in prayer, "Jesus, I cannot answer this question, and I need You to take it and give me Your comfort." When I do, He does…and I'm not the first follower of Christ who has come to Him desperate for answers, or at least for peace.

In Luke 24:38, Jesus asked His disciples, "Why are you troubled, and why do doubts arise in your hearts?"

The situation then was that, on the first Sunday morning after Jesus was crucified on Friday, His disciples discovered His tomb was empty and His body missing. Despair, fear, doubt, and puzzlement swirled in their minds. Now, on Sunday evening, Jesus revealed

Himself to them, even showing them "His hands and feet" (verse 40) and eating "a piece of broiled fish...before them" (verses 42-43).

In other words, Jesus saw their sadness and in kindness came to them. I have found that He does the same for us on our road of sorrow. Time after time and day after day, we can bring to Him the specific thoughts and situations that cause us pain and ask Him to give us His comfort and peace.

It's important for us, however, to ask ourselves the question, "Are we so absorbed in our own pain that we cannot recognize His presence and touch?"

When we sense, even for a moment, an unexplainable comfort in our hearts...it comes from Him.

When a friend stops by at our most desperate time of need... that's from Him.

When we get out of bed, even though we don't think we have the strength to do it...it's because of Him.

And so is every other moment of survival, perseverance, progress, or victory. They all come from His hand, kindly extended toward us. It's good for us to look into the blur of our days of grief and find ways that God has met us, even if we didn't realize it at the time.

It is still hard for me to understand completely why grief is so difficult to walk through. Sometimes I don't immediately understand how the awful things that happen in our lives "work together for good" (Romans 8:28). There are many times when, though the veil into God's presence is torn in two, I bump up against the fact that, for now, I "see in a mirror dimly" and "know in part" (1 Corinthians 13:12).

So it's no wonder that one of the first words that comes from the mouths of those confronted by the death of someone they love is, "Why?"

That is just fine.

The words that came from Jesus' mouth as He hung on the cross were, "My God, My God, why have You forsaken Me?" (Matthew 27:46).

If Jesus—who was God in the flesh—asked that question, don't you think God understands when we cry out the same question in our own pain? None of us will ever experience the supreme pain of Christ as He took our sins on Himself on the cross. But we can find comfort and hope in looking to the One who shed His blood for us. He knows the same deep darkness that we experience in our grief. He knows how difficult it can be for us to function when grief shatters our world. He waits for us to put our deepest needs and sorrows at His feet.

So, go ahead—ask God all the questions you want and cry as many tears as you need to cry. Jesus understands. We may not get all our questions answered this side of heaven…but until we do He will hold us in His steadying, strengthening hand.

Then, one blessed day, we will see clearly how all the pieces in the puzzle of our lives fit together.

We'll also see those who, by faith in Him, have gone before us into His presence. Praise His name!

PART 2

THE CIRCUMSTANCE: GRIEF

So…God calls us to hope.

This hope is not just wishful thinking or a manufactured illusion. Rather, it is a settled confidence based on the objective fact and enduring truth of what God's Son, the Lord Jesus Christ, has done for us.

Through Christ, we—and our griefs—have an audience in the very presence of God Himself. He loves us and, in His perfect wisdom and compassion, will help us with what we're going through here and now.

But what *about* this circumstance you're facing?

Why is it so hard, and why *does* it hurt so much?

Is what you're experiencing "normal"?

Has anybody else ever felt this way?

Is your situation somehow beyond God's help?

Is there meaning and purpose in it all?

Will things *ever* "get better"?

Let's face these questions head-on. After all, grief makes us deal "straight up," doesn't it? It makes us consider matters and talk about subjects that people not walking through grief usually avoid—glib clichés and easy answers no longer satisfy us when we're living with the "amputation" from our lives of someone who has been precious to us.

So…let's continue talking honestly as fellow travelers in grief… and in hope.

4

The Meaning of Grief

SIMPLY PUT, grief can be defined as pain caused by loss.
Some dictionaries describe it as "mental" pain or anguish, but anyone who has truly grieved knows that grief's effects are not just mental. They are physical, emotional, relational, and spiritual—in other words, they completely envelop your life. And while marked by common elements, each person's grief is unique.

One boy experienced grief early in his childhood. When he was four, his beloved dog Jacksie was hit by a car and died. This event so shook the boy's young world that soon afterward he declared his own name to be Jacksie and began responding only to that name. Eventually, he accepted the shorter version—Jack—which stuck with him the rest of his life.

Then, at the age of nine, cancer claimed the life of Jack's mother. The trauma of her death was compounded for him by the fact that his father, wading through his own grief, was not very warm or nurturing. He sent Jack to a boarding school, where his experience wasn't especially positive. However, he did become a voracious reader, finding himself entertained and intrigued in the imaginary realms of fiction.

As a teen, Jack began to weigh against the backdrop of his sorrow the Christian faith that had been taught to him as a child. With his developing keen intellect, he determined himself to be an atheist.

Having settled that matter (or so he supposed), he continued pursuing his education, pausing only to serve in the military. There, he was wounded in combat, and some of his friends were killed.

During college, Jack developed friendships with several students whose academic interests were similar to his own. Some of them were Christians. Through their influence (and quite reluctantly), he began a spiritual journey that took him from atheism to an uncertain agnosticism, then to a belief in God, and finally to personal faith in Jesus Christ.

Even as a Christian, however, Jack knew heartache. Remaining single until his late fifties, he wed a woman who died of cancer after just four years of marriage.

The rest of this story, though, is that during the 32 years between his conversion to Christ and his own death, Jack—better known to the world as C.S. Lewis—became one of the twentieth century's premier scholars, authors, and Christian apologists. His writings following the death of his wife, Joy Gresham, became the classic work *A Grief Observed*

In *A Grief Observed*, Lewis related his struggles and reflections in dealing with what his stepson called "the emotional paralysis of the most shattering grief of his life.[1] Some of his observations are timeless:

> "No one ever told me that grief felt so like fear."

> "There is a sort of invisible blanket between the world and me. I find it hard to take in what anyone says."

"I not only live each endless day in grief, but live each day thinking about living each day in grief."

"Grief still feels like fear. Perhaps, more strictly, like suspense. Or like waiting; just hanging about waiting for something to happen. It gives life a permanently provisional feeling."

"There is spread over everything a vague sense of wrongness, of something amiss."

"Does grief finally subside into boredom tinged by faint nausea?"[2]

These and other insights of Lewis's have struck familiar chords for many grieving people—including Glenda and me, which is ironically comforting.

Even more comforting to us has been the perspective on grief found in God's Word. Why does grief even exist, anyway? The Bible reveals that grief is rooted in the Garden.

In the Garden of Eden—where, according to the book of Genesis, God placed our parents Adam and Eve "in the beginning"— grief began when Adam and Eve disobeyed God. The Bible calls this sin. In the words of the apostle Paul: "Through one man sin entered into the world, and death through sin, and so death spread to all men, because all sinned" (Romans 5:12).

Consequences came with that sin-choice: separation from God… a life on earth filled with the heartaches that go along with being separated from God…and, after physical death, an eternity of misery, separated from God in a place the Bible calls hell. In a very real sense, life itself became a story of grief, marred by the pain of separation and loss rather than consisting of the perfect well-being that abounds in intimate fellowship with our Creator.

Adam and Eve quickly found this out. For starters, in the aftermath of their sin an animal had to die so that, in the shame of their nakedness, they could be clothed with its skin. Then they were cast out of the Garden and separated from the relationship with God they originally enjoyed. Their son Abel soon died, murdered by his jealous brother, Cain. Eventually they too died.

In my imagination, the epitaph on their graves reads, "If only…"

As subsequent generations unfolded, God Himself "was grieved in His heart" as He "saw that the wickedness of man was great on the earth, and that every intent of the thoughts of his heart was only evil continually. The LORD was sorry that He had made man on the earth" (Genesis 6:5-6).

At this point, I'm sure you're asking, "So where is the comfort in all of this?"

Please stick with me.

As we've seen, grief is rooted in the Garden…but hope comes through the cross.

It was on the cross, where the sinless Son of God, the Lord Jesus Christ, paid the penalty of sin even though He Himself did not owe it, that reconciliation rather than separation and hope rather than despair became an alternative for us. In Christ, death no longer has to be the final summation of our lives.

Paul declared, "For the wages of sin is death, but the free gift of God is eternal life in Christ Jesus our Lord" (Romans 6:23).

The New Testament writer to the Hebrews said, "We do see Him…namely, Jesus, because of the suffering of death crowned with glory and honor, so that by the grace of God He might taste death for everyone" (Hebrews 2:9).

We'll see a bit later that death on the cross wasn't the end for the Lord Jesus, but for now consider this: grief is really a commemoration of the way God designed things to be before sin entered the world. Sin resulted in separation between God and us and, as a result, between others and us. Our groaning over death is a testimony to the awfulness of sin in the human race, which is where that pain of separation from those we love, and who love us, comes from.

A number of years ago, the relationship between C.S. Lewis and his wife was portrayed in a movie called *Shadowlands*. In one scene, he and Joy discuss the sorrow that will soon be his after she succumbs to the cancer in her body. She tells him, "The pain then is part of the happiness now. That's the deal."

Her statement acknowledges the intertwining of grief and love with which we currently live. It underscores that grief exists because sin produced death, and death brings separation and loss to loving relationships. For now, the two go hand in hand.

In the movie, after Joy dies, Lewis recalls her words and relates them to a young student who asks the question, "Why love if losing hurts so much?"

Lewis responds, "The pain now is part of the happiness then. That's the deal."

The amazing good news of the Bible is that Almighty God Himself loved us so much that He was willing to endure the pain of His one and only Son's death so that our separation from Him could be remedied, we could be rescued, and that which has been lost to sin could be restored.

In this world we cannot avoid pain caused by loss, but through Christ we are offered the hope of facing and passing through it with the comfort and peace that He alone can give. There's no better time for you to embrace it than right now, in the midst of your grief.

Have you?

Will you?

From Glenda…Our Times

A time to weep, and a time to laugh…
ECCLESIASTES 3:4

Standing in the kitchen…

The noise was startling.

I do not know how long I had been standing by my kitchen sink, but my trance was broken by the noise of my own sighs. At that moment I grasped what the Bible means when it speaks of "groanings too deep for words" (Romans 8:26).

Grief is an experience that we enter into and endure for long periods—maybe a lifetime. It is a state of the heart that we do not "get over." Rather, we learn to live it. We wear it.

After someone dies, outsiders commonly say, "Life goes on." That is true.

However, for those who suffer loss, life will not ever go on the same as it did before. We must learn how to move forward with a constant ache in our hearts.

This morning, I read of a mother whose son died at war. He had been killed several years earlier, and she was still wading through grief. Her story was in the news because she was fighting a battle with the United States government to be buried with her son in a national cemetery. When asked about her request, she said this:

> It [her son's death] was the most devastating blow that
> I could ever get. I miss him so much. Just being with
> him will give me some sort of peace. Every day I wake

up and I look at his pictures and I cry. It doesn't get any
easier. Maybe down the road I will be able to deal with
it a little bit better, but right now, it is not easy.[3]

In her own way, she was trying to learn how to go on with life
while having this pain in her heart.

Before I experienced the loss of my own child, I knew many
people who had lost spouses, siblings, and children to death. Sadly,
I must admit that I thought they would return to their "normal"
life after a brief time. Now I know what an ignorant and absurd assumption that was on my part. I've experienced firsthand that, once
you have a child, he or she is intertwined through every facet of your
life. When that child dies, your life is never the "normal" you once
knew it to be.

This became a stark reality to me as I tried to return to somewhat normal days after Nathan's death. I would be doing the most
routine activity in my house, and then I would run across something Nathan had written or something he had made. I would
open a drawer, and there staring at me would be a reminder of
him. I would open a closet and there before me would be another
reminder. I would look in a box and there would be a toy he had
played with as a child, or a photo of a fun day sometime during the
course of his life.

Sigh…sigh…sigh.

I missed him, and I also found myself grieving the dreams I had
for him.

While carrying a child or waiting for completion of the adop-
tion process, it is natural to constantly think of that new little person who will be entering your life, even before you know whether
you're having a boy or girl. You make plans, prepare a room, choose

a name, and daydream of how much you love that little one, even before you know him or her.

Once you hold that heavenly gift in your arms, you begin to discover his or her every trait, the amazing intricacy with which he or she has been created, and very quickly, a developing personality. You learn the things that uniquely interest your children. Their joys become your joys, their hurts become your hurts.

Your life becomes identified, at least in some measure, with theirs. As you invest your time and love, you naturally begin to en-vision what the rest of their lives will hold.

When your child dies, it is difficult to let go of the excitement you had for the rest of his or her life. You grieve a dream that can never come to pass.

Jesus understands the experience of grief. He Himself grieved. The Bible says in Matthew 26:37-38: "He...began to be grieved and distressed. Then He said to them, 'My soul is deeply grieved to the point of death.'"

When Jesus considered He was facing death on the cross so He could bear the penalty for your sins and mine, He began to grieve. It was not just a fleeting moment of sadness but the full experience of grief such as no one else has ever known. While we will never go through the intense darkness and pain that Jesus experienced, it brings comfort to know that He understands our grief completely.

Maybe you have lost someone you love to cancer or another ill-ness, an accident, a natural disaster, murder, or suicide. Maybe your brave loved one has given his or her life for the cause of freedom. Whatever the particular chain of events has been for you, your heart is grieving.

Jesus knows.

He sees your tears and broken heart.

He understands the experience of grief you're dealing
minute of every single day.

He will give you His comfort if you'll cast your cares upon Him.

After all, as your loving heavenly Father, "He cares for you affectionately and cares about you watchfully" (1 Peter 5:7 AMP).

Amazingly, your life is intertwined with His.

5

The Magnitude of Grief

A SURGEON FRIEND once said to me, "Minor surgery is when a procedure happens to someone else. Major surgery is when it happens to me!"

He was only half joking, and yet he captured (sort of) a truth expressed in Scripture:

> The heart knows its own bitterness,
> And a stranger does not share its joy (Proverbs 14:10).

What each of us goes through is personal to us. *Our* tragedies are a big deal to *us,* whether or not anyone else recognizes them. Our grief affects us personally in real and large ways, even if tragedies that others experience seem—from an outsider's perspective—to be much greater.

Consider events that occurred in September 2001, for example. During that month, countless people in the United States and beyond experienced emotional and physical trauma through automobile accidents, medical conditions, job losses, divorces, crimes, and other circumstances. Each affected individual's turmoil was real, in many cases scarring them for the rest of their lives.

However, during that same month:

- A tornado ripped through Virginia and Maryland and killed 3 people

- Two explosions at an Alabama coal mine killed 13 people

- A fire in a club in Tokyo, Japan, killed 44 people

- A typhoon caused 79 deaths in Taiwan

- A chemical plant explosion in France damaged some 20,000 buildings, killed 29 people, and injured more than 2500[1]

Of course, on September 11, 2001, terrorists hijacked four U.S. aircraft, crashing them into New York City's World Trade Center, the Pentagon in Washington, DC, and a Pennsylvania field. The number of people dead or missing totaled nearly 3000. The event stunned millions of Americans, as well as multitudes across the globe, forever altering our collective sense of security and perception of the world.

But…in these events during the month of September 2001, whose grief was "worse"? Was it the grief of the person who received a dire medical diagnosis from a doctor, or the one who was handed divorce papers from a spouse, or perhaps the one who was brutalized by an attacker?

Was it the grief of the person whose loved one died in a natural disaster, or the grief of the person whose loved one died in a humanly caused event such as war, murder, or suicide?

Was it the grief of the person whose loved one died in \ or Maryland? In Japan? In Taiwan? In Alabama? In France? Or in New York, Washington, or Pennsylvania?

While the events themselves had varying degrees of impact on society as a whole, the case can be made that the impact for each grieving person was potentially, for him or her at that moment, just as great as anyone else's. Any tragedy, whatever the circumstance, will devastate someone. To declare otherwise would be insensitive, if not uncaring.

However, we must also acknowledge that tragedy and grief are like earthquakes—they do come in varying magnitudes. Quakes of lower level magnitudes resulting in repairable damage are certainly real and unsettling, but they pale in comparison with quakes of catastrophic magnitudes that wreak irreparable devastation—like the massive quake that struck Haiti in January 2010, destroying much of the country's infrastructure, displacing over a million Haitians, and killing at least 200,000 people.

In our family, before Nathan died, we had experienced "lower magnitude" events that tore at our hearts and drove us to our knees in prayer in order to survive them. Those were the worst storms we had encountered to the moment. But then...

The point is this: true hope must be sufficient across the full range of grief's magnitudes. It must be relevant and viable in every situation we face. It can't just help in "smaller" situations, only to wear thin and evaporate in "larger" ones. True hope is found in Christ alone.

Such hope—hope that could transcend and triumph over any and every tragedy, whatever its magnitude—was what carried Job through his deep darkness. From the very depths of his pain, he declared:

As for me, I know that my Redeemer lives,
And at the last He will take His stand on the earth.
Even after my skin is destroyed,
Yet from my flesh I shall see God;
Whom I myself shall behold,
And whom my eyes will see and not another
   (Job 19:25-27).

Job had this insight even though he lived hundreds of years before Christ was born, died, and then conquered the grave. Today, we have the benefit of looking back on these events, which occurred in history some 2000 years ago.

We can have this hope knowing that "our Lord Jesus Christ Himself and God our Father…has loved us and given us eternal comfort and good hope by grace" and that God does indeed desire to "comfort and strengthen [our] hearts" (2 Thessalonians 2:16-17).

The hope of Christ is an anchor that holds and helps us not only across the spectrum of grief-causing events that can befall us, but also throughout the course of our grieving. And grieving does unfold over time, in different ways as time progresses.

In recent decades, psychiatrists and others have done a great deal of research and writing on various aspects of grief. Some of the findings have certainly contributed to an increased awareness and understanding of grief's dynamics. This material is widely available for persons wanting to study it.

However, we are writing not as clinical observers of grief but as travelers through it. In our experience, grief is not a paint-by-number exercise that precisely follows a script. Rather, it unfolds in varying ways and on varying timetables for each individual. And it does seem to have something of a time-release effect to it.

You've seen advertisements for medications that are ~~products. They provide an initial surge of effect soon a~~ taken and then a more measured seep of effect over time.

For us, that's how grief has happened. We've experienced initially shocking effects…we've experienced subsequent effects that, while of more moderate intensity, have been nonetheless real and continuing…and now, some years after Nathan's death, we continue to experience permanent effects that will go with us through the rest of our days. We've talked with others for whom this is true as well.

We don't believe—either for us or for you—that this time-release dynamic is good or bad, that it's a symptom of strength or weakness, or that it's spiritual or unspiritual—it's just the way it is. Having the hope of Christ in our hearts, however, is what makes all the difference in how we walk through grief, whatever magnitude of event we may be facing.

That is "strong encouragement to take hold of the hope set before us" (Hebrews 6:18).

From Glenda…Our Times

A time to be silent…

ECCLESIASTES 3:7

Silence is often more powerful than noise.

Immediately following Nathan's death, silence would take my heart and mind into uncharted territory day after day. Sometimes this was terrifying. However, I began to find that in silence God would speak to my heart and provide comfort and direction.

One day as Preston and I talked about all the events that had occurred, he told me Nathan had been reading a different chapter of Proverbs each morning since January 1. I immediately turned in my Bible to Proverbs 24, the chapter he would have read on the morning of January 24, the day he fell to his death.

This passage reinforced that God's Word really is living. I loved being able to identify with Nathan as I clung to each word in the chapter. Then, it was as if one verse leapt off the page and spoke with clarity and power to my heart personally:

> If you are slack in the day of distress,
> Your strength is limited (Proverbs 24:10).

The magnitude of my circumstance had paralyzed me until that moment. The power of God's Word was intimately speaking to me and steering me in a direction that required action on my part. When I read these words, I knew God was making it clear I could not live out the rest of my days without the strength that comes from clinging to Jesus.

When faced with the devastation of grief, I found it easy to become isolated, fearful, and slack, especially when it took every bit of strength I could muster just to get out of bed in the morning, put one foot in front of the other, and get dressed.

Reading this verse gave me the perspective I needed, which started with calling on Jesus even before I got out of bed in the morning. I began asking Him to help me and hold me up so I could get through that day. The next thing I knew, I wanted to come out of each day stronger than the day before. It gave me purpose.

From the outset, Preston and I decided together that we wanted to come through our grief strong. When we made that decision,

I did not know exactly what it meant. I was operating in survival mode and with tunnel vision in order to get to the end of each day. Gaining strength was the last thing I was focusing on.

Maybe you don't feel very strong right now. If not, just getting through today will be an accomplishment of strength. Then tomorrow, wake up in the morning, call out to Jesus, and ask Him to get you through another day. He will strengthen you once more.

Strength comes through reading the Bible. In the early days after Nathan's death, Isaiah 43:2 was especially helpful to me: "When you pass through the waters, I will be with you; and through the rivers, they will not overflow you. When you walk through the fire, you will not be scorched, nor will the flame burn you."

The power of these words still brings me much strength and comfort. At times, I have felt as if I were in deep waters and my eyeballs were just barely above the surface. Whenever I feel like I am about to drown in sorrow or be overcome by despair, I get my Bible, sit down in silence, and read this verse.

God always keeps His promises, and this verse refreshes my memory. It grips my heart and strengthens me to go on with my day.

It is so important in the middle of grief to have tangible things to help us get through. A friend whose son also suddenly died told me how important it was for her that one person called her every single day. Praise God, I had one of those faithful friends too. Of course, God's Word is always available to us and is the most obvious place to turn when we do not know how we will make it through another day.

You may be at a point in your grief right now where you feel so broken that nothing comforts or even interests you. God knows. *He cares.* He will strengthen your heart if you turn to Him. If right now you can't even pick up your Bible, perhaps in your own silence you can begin moving forward by clinging to this verse: "My flesh and my heart may fail, but God is the strength of my heart" (Psalm 73:26).

The effects of grief are consuming. We're never quite sure what the next day will hold. I have spent so many days feeling as if I were trapped inside a box or as if I were wearing something uncomfortable that I desperately wanted to get out of but couldn't. Though those feelings have lessened, when they come, they come in waves.

My confidence is that God will continue to strengthen me through each of those moments as they arise. I know He will, because He has told me He will—His Word says so.

That is a hope that does not disappoint.

PART 3

THE CERTAINTY: GOD'S DEED AND WORD

Some time ago, I had one of those landmark birthdays... you know, one that changes the first number of the two you cite when asked how old you are.

Family members and friends were, of course, happy to join in gloating over...er, celebrating...the occasion. One way they did so was to present me with a personal-sized cake, thickly iced and topped by a flaming candle.

I was touched by their thoughtfulness and, after blowing out the candle, willingly complied when they urged me to take a bite. After all, it looked so sweet and delicious— why just stare at it?

My taste buds watering, I plunged a fork into it, captured a hunk of it, and shoved it in my mouth. As I bit down, however, I immediately realized something was wrong. Rather than the cake under the icing consisting of the usual finely mixed, perfectly baked flour and other ingredients, it was made of only one thing—shortening!

That's right—these special individuals…these stellar examples of the treasure of friendship…these people representing the highest and best assets accrued over the course of my increasing years…on this tender occasion calling for all the sensitivity, affirmation, and encouragement they could offer—fed me shortening!

It wasn't enough for them that I was now entering an era of life in which I was statistically more likely to keel over anyway—they apparently wanted to help the process along by filling my arteries with a dose of cholesterol!

Gee…what friends…thanks!

As I spit it out, we all had a good laugh. I appreciated their effort to cheer me up on a day that could have been depressing.

When it comes to the subject we're dealing with, however—finding hope in the midst of grief—we don't want to encounter any such surprises, or rather, disappointments.

Samuel Johnson said, "That hope only is rational of which we are certain that it cannot deceive us."[1]

We need assurance that the hope God offers us in Christ doesn't consist merely of a superficial coating of sweetness smeared on a foundation with no enduring substance. We don't want to come up short!

What, after all, is the basis of certainty for this hope we're considering? What makes it more than just wishful thinking, just a concoction for people who are hurting and desperately need some sort of consolation, whether or not it's true?

It's time for us to focus on two indispensable pillars of hope—the resurrection of Christ and the Word of God.

6

The Resurrection of Christ

"H E HAS RISEN" (Matthew 28:6).

The resurrection of Jesus Christ is the most profound event in all of history. Announced by an angel in the simplest of words to the mourning women who came to Christ's tomb, its importance cannot be overstated. Our hope—whether in times of grief, or at any other time—absolutely hinges upon it. Christ's resurrection is the sole basis for our consolation and hope.

Why is this so?

First, Christ's resurrection announced that His sacrifice for our sins was ample and acceptable in God's sight. The apostle Paul, who had originally opposed and persecuted believers in Christ but who came to see the truth about Him, said, "If Christ has not been raised, your faith is worthless; you are still in your sins...But now Christ has been raised from the dead" (1 Corinthians 15:17,20).

When faced with the loss of a loved one or with our own impending death, we have no greater need than the assurance that their sins, and ours, are forgiven. Through Christ God has made forgiveness and assurance available to anyone who will turn away from their sins and believe in Him with childlike faith. The knowledge that our son Nathan had done so has helped to make his death and absence more bearable.

Second, Christ's resurrection demonstrated the fact that He is indeed Lord. Preaching boldly to the throngs assembled in Jerusalem for the Jewish feast of Pentecost, just weeks after Christ was crucified, the apostle Peter declared: "This Jesus God raised up again, to which we are all witnesses…Therefore let all the house of Israel know for certain that God has made Him both Lord and Christ—this Jesus whom you crucified" (Acts 2:32,36).

Faced with issues of life and death and heaven and hell, there is no one higher or even equal on whom we can rely for our eternal well-being. Only Jesus is Lord.

Third, Christ's resurrection marked the defeat of death, which no longer has to have the last word over us. The last book of the Bible opens with this declaration from Christ Himself: "Do not be afraid; I am the first and the last, and the living One; and I was dead, and behold, I am alive forevermore, and I have the keys of death and of Hades" (Revelation 1:17-18).

Peter said at Pentecost:

> Men of Israel, listen to these words: Jesus the Nazarene, a man attested to you by God with miracles and wonders and signs which God performed through Him in your midst, just as you yourselves know—this Man, delivered over by the predetermined plan and foreknowledge of God, you nailed to a cross by the hands of godless men and put Him to death. But God raised Him up again, putting an end to the agony of death,

since it was impossible for Him to be held in its power
(Acts 2:22-24).

Paul wrote to the Romans, "We shall also live with Him, knowing that Christ, having been raised from the dead, is never to die again; death no longer is master over Him" (Romans 6:8-9).

Fourth, Christ's resurrection moves us beyond dead memories, good as they may be, to living hope. The apostle Peter emphasized this in his first New Testament letter:

> Blessed be the God and Father of our Lord Jesus Christ,
> who according to His great mercy has caused us to be
> born again to a living hope through the resurrection of
> Jesus Christ from the dead, to obtain an inheritance
> which is imperishable and undefiled and will not fade
> away, reserved in heaven for you (1 Peter 1:3-4).

In the weeks following that fateful call we received about Nathan, many well-intentioned people urged us to find solace in our memories of him. To some degree that was helpful, and we do have many fond memories of his time with us for which we are grateful. However, true consolation requires more than memories. In fact, memories alone can intensify the pain of a loved one's death and haunt rather than console us. Christ's resurrection moves us beyond dead memories to living hope—hope of seeing our believing loved ones again and, more importantly, hope of dwelling for all eternity in the glorious presence of the Lord Jesus Christ Himself.

Fifth, Christ's resurrection holds the only resolution for so many of the regrets, injustices, and mysteries that life in a fallen world inevitably involves. If we're honest, all of us struggle with those things in one way or another. The only way we can stare them in the face and not become distracted, absorbed, and overcome by these here-and-now struggles is by looking ahead to the day when all who are Christ's followers will, in the words of Paul, "attain to the resurrection from the dead":

> Not that I have already obtained it or have already become perfect, but I press on so that I may lay hold of that for which also I was laid hold of by Christ Jesus. Brethren, I do not regard myself as having laid hold of it yet; but one thing I do: forgetting what lies behind and reaching forward to what lies ahead, I press on toward the goal for the prize of the upward call of God in Christ Jesus. Let us therefore, as many as are perfect, have this attitude (Philippians 3:12-15).

Because Christ lives, hope is not merely wishful thinking or some manufactured illusion. It isn't a fantasy on which we fixate in order to mystically influence events or at least to make ourselves feel better. It depends not on our fickle emotions, or on ritual or chance, but on God, and on what He has done in Christ. True biblical hope is a settled confidence based on the objective, historic fact of His victory over the grave.

If, for you, the fact of Christ's resurrection is a serious question that hinders you from embracing the hope He offers, face your concerns and sincerely study the evidence for it—it is abundant.[1] We're confident that doing so will put this issue to rest for you. In fact, some have called the resurrection of Christ the best-attested fact in history.

For us, putting this issue to rest in our minds has been vital to having rest and hope in our hearts as we walk through our times of grief.

From Glenda…Our Times

A time to tear down and a time to build up…
ECCLESIASTES 3:3

Six of us piled into our Suburban early on Easter morning.
We were silent.
I felt empty.
After what seemed like a long road trip, we finally arrived at the local cemetery where Nathan's body was buried. We slowly made the dreaded walk to his grave.

A year earlier, no one would have ever thought that this would be our first activity on our next Easter morning together.

We stood in silence, and then Preston began to read Scripture. I kept my eyes fixed on the ground in which our precious son had been laid to rest. I could hear sniffles—my other children also had their eyes fixed on the ground under which their brother's body lay.

At that moment, all of us could feel in the air the realness of death like never before. Then, though, the Lord spoke to my heart: *Glenda, I was resurrected from the dead.*

At once, the meaning of what we were to celebrate that Easter morning overcame me, and I learned two things.

First, I realized that the emptiness I felt on the way to the cemetery and upon our arrival must have been similar to the emptiness that Jesus' mother, Mary, and also Mary Magdalene felt as they stood together at Jesus' tomb. The Bible says, "Mary [Magdalene] was standing outside the tomb weeping; and so, as she wept, she stooped and looked into the tomb" (John 20:11).

There is a difference, however, between their visit to the tomb and ours when we go to the grave of someone we love. When they looked into the tomb that first Easter morning, it was empty.

Think of it—*a tomb in which the body of Jesus had been laid, now empty!*

They did not stand there blankly staring at lifeless ground. They gazed at the proof that the very One who came to give us Life was resurrected. What they saw changed history, and changed our lives, forever.

Second, Mary Magdalene loved Jesus because He had transformed her life of sin and aimlessness into a life of newness and purpose. I personally have known that kind of transformation in my own life.

In addition to being a literal, historic fact, the resurrection of Christ is a powerful picture of what God has done in me. My own mother will say to this day that the gloomy teenager she knew so well was transformed into one with a light in her eye and a fresh spring in her step once she—I—made a commitment to follow Jesus. He gave me new life. This was possible because He Himself was resurrected. His resurrection gave my life a power that it did not have without Him.

If you have entered into a personal relationship with Christ, you too have experienced the power of the resurrection, even before that coming day when your body will be transformed. However, if you are one of many who have not yet made that wonderful discovery, I want to stop right here and say that you can. Pray right now. Ask God to forgive your sins because of what Christ did. Ask Him to come into your heart and life, and tell Him you want to follow Him.

Once you do, you will no longer be traveling the road of grief alone. Jesus will walk with you every step of the way.

There is a certain ache to realizing that the death of a loved one is final. It is hard to swallow the fact they will not be coming through the door anymore to say, "Hey, Mom!"…or coming home from a business trip to tell you that they missed you…or returning from their latest, greatest adventure excited to tell you every detail. It hurts, and there is just no way to get around it.

However, what was reinforced in my life that Easter morning is that the emptiness we felt in that sad moment was not actually the final word. The reason is that we—and Nathan—know the One who rose from the dead.

The Bible says Jesus "was declared the Son of God with power by the resurrection from the dead, according to the spirit of holiness" (Romans 1:4).

No one else in this world has conquered the grave. Even the people Jesus raised during His earthly ministry subsequently returned to the grave. Not one of us can cause a person or thing that is truly dead to become permanently alive. But God brought His Son, Jesus, back to life as a demonstration to us of the power that we are able to share as believers in Him. That definitely gives us hope.

A few days after Nathan died, my cousin Julia sent me a lette She wrote that, as she prayed, she felt impressed that Nathan di' suffer any pain as he fell and that angels immediately ush into heaven. Our funeral director, who did not know o' letter, also told us that, from what he could see, he b transition to heaven happened in an instant.

I will not know until I get to heaven ing words are true. However, I am tha Word that Nathan did indeed trans on that day.

Therefore, being always of good courage, and knowing that while we are at home in the body we are absent from the Lord—for we walk by faith, not by sight—we are of good courage, I say, and prefer rather to be absent from the body and to be at home with the Lord (2 Corinthians 5:6-8).

Once Nathan was received into heaven, he had no pain and began experiencing a fullness that comes only from the resurrected One.

The power of life in Jesus enables me to raise my eyes from the grave and gives me the assurance—the hope—that I will see Nathan again. That Easter morning as I sat in church, I could worship more intensely and sing a little louder because I knew in an even deeper way the One we were praising.

I understood as never before the power of His resurrection.

It is that power that will sustain me the rest of my days on this earth until I too arrive safely home with Him.

7

The Word of God

IT'S ONE OF MY MOST cherished possessions.

The "it" I'm referring to is a three-page, handwritten letter, sent to me by Nathan on Father's Day four years before he died. In it, Nathan wrote "a few reasons why my father is someone that I admire and respect" (kindness was always one of his attributes). He said, "As I live and learn, and grow, I am beginning to realize what it is to be a man…and I know that to be a man is to be something like my father."

Thankfully, Nathan went on during his remaining time here to focus even more on His heavenly Father, and on allowing God to make him a man of God who was becoming increasingly more like His Son, the Lord Jesus Christ.

To this day, however, I keep that letter, in its original envelope, inside the cover of one of my Bibles. It meant a great deal to me when I first received it, and now—obviously—it is irreplaceable.

This particular letter was one of a number that, in an age of computers, printers, and email, Nathan wrote out longhand, and then put into an envelope, stamped, and mailed. Each of Nathan's letters demonstrated his thoughtfulness and sincerity, and blessed whoever was fortunate enough to receive it. For others in our family and beyond, some of his writings have become keepsakes which we refer to over and over, filled with insights that are still of great importance.

Rereading one of Nathan's letters is, for me, not just a reminder of what he said—it's a fresh encounter with who he was. As I read his words, I "hear" his voice, "see" his face, and experience his heart. When I stop to think about it, I'm amazed that characters written in ink on paper can not only communicate a message, but can also convey something of a person's very essence in a way that continues to have powerful effects even though he is no longer here.

I realize this experience has been at the heart of writing since it began in its most primitive forms thousands of years ago—it's just that I've experienced it very personally in relation to Nathan since his death. Maybe you've had a similar experience when reading something written by your own deceased loved one, whether from your father or mother, brother or sister, child or grandchild, or friend.[1]

It is this same principle—that written characters can not only communicate a message but also convey the very essence of who a person is—that applies when we deal with the Word of God, the Bible. In fact, God's Word is like no other book in the world.

The Bible isn't just people's writings *about* God. It is actually *from* God Himself, who took the initiative to impart to the world the enduring truth about His Son, the Lord Jesus Christ—before He came, while He was here, and since He departed.[2] It's no coincidence that, when Christ appeared, He did so as "the Word" who "became flesh, and dwelt among us" with "glory as of the only begotten from the Father, full of grace and truth" (John 1:14).

Given over some 1500 years through 40 or so different writers, the words of the 66 books of the Old and New Testaments were actually "God breathed" (the literal meaning of "inspired" in 2 Timothy 3:16-17) as the Holy Spirit moved in the hearts and minds of the writers. The result is unparalleled.

Jesus Himself said in prayer to His heavenly Father, "Your word is truth" (John 17:17).

He also said, "Heaven and earth will pass away, but My words will not pass away" (Matthew 24:35).

The apostle Peter, quoting the Old Testament prophet Isaiah, wrote:

> All flesh is like grass,
> And all its glory like the flower of grass.
> The grass withers,
> And the flower falls off,
> But the word of the Lord endures forever
> (1 Peter 1:24-25).

The writer of the New Testament book of Hebrews declared, "The word of God is living and active and sharper than any two-edged sword, and piercing to the division of soul and of spirit, of both joints and marrow, and able to judge the thoughts and intentions of the heart" (Hebrews 4:12).

The Bible is not merely a book of legends, sayings, and moral teachings. It is the one book in all of history that is accurately and authoritatively the Truth, and that reveals to us everything we need to know to be saved from our sins and to receive eternal life. Ancient manuscripts, archaeological findings, and world events uniquely validate it. More people have read it, in more languages, than any other book in history.

So what does all this have to do with finding hope in our grief?

Quite simply, everything.

"Whatever was written in earlier times was written for our instruction, so that through perseverance and the encouragement of the Scriptures we might have hope," said the apostle Paul (Romans 15:4).

The Word of God is an unchanging, immoveable pillar of our hope, one that is not subject to the roller coaster of emotions that marks our times of grief.

The Word of God is the rock-solid foundation that enables a "house"—namely, your life or mine—to withstand the awful storms that assail us through the loss of a loved one. It alone is what can infuse us with comfort, perspective, and strength in the midst of these storms. Jesus talked about this as He concluded His Sermon on the Mount in Matthew 7:24-25:

> Therefore everyone who hears these words of Mine and acts on them, may be compared to a wise man who built his house on the rock. And the rain fell, and the floods came, and the winds blew and slammed against that house; and yet it did not fall, for it had been founded on the rock.

If, for you, the reliability of God's Word is a serious question that hinders you from embracing the hope God offers, face your concerns and sincerely study the evidence for it. As with the evidence for His resurrection, we're confident that doing so will put this issue to rest for you, as it has for millions of others.[3] After all:

> God is not a man, that He should lie,
> Nor a son of man, that He should repent;
> Has He said, and will He not do it?
> Or has He spoken, and will He not make
>   it good? (Numbers 23:19).

As I said at the outset of this chapter, I cherish Nathan's letter and read it from time to time. However, God's letter—the Bible—is infinitely greater than anything any of us could ever write. It was the Word of God that changed Nathan's heart and life, readying him by the time of his death for entrance into heaven.

That's why, on his grave marker, we had inscribed a portion of God's Word that summed up the faith in which Nathan came to rest:

> He alone is my rock and my salvation;
> he is my fortress, I will not be shaken.
> My salvation and my honor depend on God;
> he is my mighty rock, my refuge
> (Psalm 62: 5-7 NIV).

May we too "hold fast the confession of our hope without wavering, for He who promised is faithful" (Hebrews 10:23).

From Glenda…Our Times

A time to search…

ECCLESIASTES 3:6

Each morning, the first thing I must do after my feet hit the floor is open my Bible and read a portion. By looking into God's Word, I'm able to see more of the One who is my life.

The Bible is like water to my thirsty soul. I so understand the psalmist who wrote: "As the deer pants for the water brooks, so my soul pants for You, O God" (Psalm 42:1).

I too must have a drink from heaven before I start my day, in order to make it through that day with perspective and power. This has been true for more than 35 years…and it was the only place I knew to turn within minutes of the news of Nathan's death.

The night we learned of Nathan's fatal accident, our friends Mel and Terri came to our house to be with us. As we all sat on the couch in our living room, not knowing what to say, I asked Mel to read Scripture. We had some Scripture verse cards in a box nearby, so someone grabbed those and handed them to him.

My request may have stunned him, but he politely read, and I was comforted hearing the words of Scripture read aloud. The Bible has provided direction, words of counsel, and desperately needed comfort in my life all these years. We desperately needed a drink of water at that moment, and God's Word—read aloud—provided that for our family that night. In my initial hours of grief, it kept me from sinking into a dark abyss, perhaps never to surface again.

One of the people who came the morning after Nathan's death was a younger woman named Anna. She is like a daughter to me, and Nathan loved her like a sister. Through our hugs and tears, she handed me two verses that she had nicely mounted on blue construction paper. I hung them on my bathroom mirror and, for many days, I read those verses over and over. They gave me the drink that I needed time and time again.

Then there was Katey, a friend of our daughter, JesseRuth, who taped Scripture verses to JesseRuth's sixth grade locker on her return to school. It was a tender moment when I found out what Katey had done. God's Word encouraged JesseRuth and reassured her that God was with her as she once again began to walk the halls of her school and return to class. What a daunting act that can be in middle school, even without going through a death in the family!

God's Word is also available to you and can help you get through your difficult days. The Bible says: "Let my cry come before You, O LORD; Give me understanding according to Your Word" (Psalm 119:169).

It also says:

> Your word is a lamp to my feet,
> And a light to my path (Psalm 119:105).

While the Bible has not given me specific reasons why Nathan had to leave this earth so soon, it has given me the assurance that my son is safe with Jesus.

It has provided me with the strength to understand that God will get me through this sorrow.

It has comforted me that I will not be alone as I walk through this valley of the shadow of death.

It has also shone light on where I stand in life right now while providing the direction needed to walk when I didn't think I could take a step or even stand up.

It will do the same for you—it is God-breathed, and through it God will fill you with the breath of hope.

The night that Nathan died, I could not read the Bible myself and needed someone to read it to me. This has happened at other times as well…when I was sick, when I was in a delivery room about to give birth, the night my grandmother died, and in the days after our older son Gregory had an accident and fractured his skull. Perhaps you are at such a moment right now, when you can't even begin to think of where to turn to get comfort. Try searching the Scriptures—if you just can't focus enough to read, get someone to read to you.

Here are a few verses for starters:

> I shall lift up my hands to Your commandments,
> Which I love;
> And I will meditate on Your statutes.
> Remember the word to Your servant,
> In which You have made me hope.
> This is comfort in my affliction,
> That Your word has revived me (Psalm 119:48-50).

Also:

> Sustain me according to Your word, that I may live;
> And do not let me be ashamed of my hope
> (Psalm 119:116).

And then:

> I wait for the LORD, my soul does wait,
> And in His word do I hope (Psalm 130:5).

The power of God's Word comforts and sustains us as we walk through our days of sorrow. If you spend time in His Word, you will experience that God is indeed the God of comfort and hope.

He will walk with you throughout these days, and you will not be alone.

PART 4

THE COMFORT:
CHRIST IS WITH US

The Holy Spirit—also called the Comforter in the Bible—speaks to us about Christ (John 15:26). Before Christ died, He promised His followers that the Father would give them the Holy Spirit as a "Helper, that He may be with you forever" (John 14:16). In fact, one of the names of Christ in Scripture is Immanuel—"God with us."

His living presence, through the Holy Spirit, is what sustains us in grief.

The chapters that follow provide some glimpse of how He is with us, and how His presence comforts us.

May you grow in hope as you consider His promises to always be present with us.

8

At All Times

NATHAN LOVED TO watch the sunrise.

I remember being especially grateful for the sunrise the first time we ever went camping.

Nathan, his brother, Gregory, and I began camping together when they were small boys. Nathan was three the first time we slept in a tent. We pitched it up the mountain behind our house. It was late fall, and overnight the temperature unexpectedly dipped well below freezing. We were less than prepared.

Nathan and Gregory both slept soundly. I, on the other hand, remember spending most of the night lying awake shivering in the cold. (I'm allergic to cold weather!) I could hardly wait for the sun to rise so I could go get a hot cup of coffee.

When the sun finally did come up, it was one of the sweetest sights I'd ever seen. I was glad to have survived, and to begin thawing out. However, our sons thought camping was the greatest adventure of their young lives, and they were eager for more.

That was the first of many nights Nathan spent camping—some

with Gregory and me; some with other friends or on his own—in places ranging from the mountains of North Carolina to the eastern United States' Appalachian Trail, from remote beaches along the Atlantic Ocean and Great Lakes to Wyoming's Tetons and the precipice of Arizona's Grand Canyon…and finally, to California's San Jacinto mountains.

There, on the periphery of the camp where he was working, Nathan spent his last night on earth in the same way he had spent so many others: outdoors nestled in his sleeping bag, which he had stretched out on a thick ground pad. He relished being able to watch the stars overhead as he fell asleep.

As best as we can tell in piecing events together, on the day he died he awoke before dawn and headed up the trail toward Tahquitz so he could climb it and watch the sun come up. Had all gone as planned, he could have done that and still been back to camp in time to report for his shift.

His excitement was evident in what turned out to be his last bit of journal writing, which was recovered—along with his Bible—from the base of the route known as Open Book. He was obviously anticipating a great day, beginning it by reflecting on God's beauty as described in Psalm 19:1:

> The heavens are telling of the glory of God;
> And their expanse is declaring the work of His hands.

That day, however, Nathan went on to see beyond the heaven of the birds and the stars—he was ushered into the very dwelling place of God.

While that event represented the fulfillment of his hope, it drove our souls to the utter necessity of clinging to Christ as we continued on here without him. It made us desperately needy for the comfort of Christ at all times—at sunrise, at sunset, and at every moment in between.

It made me feel much like the psalmist must have felt as he did his own journal writing:

> I wait for the LORD, my soul does wait,
> And in His word do I hope.
> My soul waits for the Lord
> More than the watchmen for the morning;
> Indeed, more than the watchmen for
> the morning (Psalm 130:5-6).

Since Nathan died, I've never viewed sunrises and sunsets in the same way. Some time ago I shared these words with a friend whose own adult son had died unexpectedly and with whom I correspond from time to time. I wrote:

> I've just been watching the sun set here. I don't think I ever see a sunset now without seeing "past" it, as it were, and thinking of the realm where our beloved are. I long to be there with them—with Him—and in due time we shall be. For now, though, we continue through this world that's passing away with a strange perspective— you know, like the apostle Paul, who said it's better to depart and be with Christ, but for now it's profitable to be here. It'll sure be great, though, when the final trumpet sounds and we get to go home.

Now, well over a thousand sunrises and sunsets later, we can testify that waiting for the Lord and hoping in His Word are not in vain. We've endured many long nights, but we have experienced for ourselves that while "weeping may last for the night," even in times of grief it really can be true that "joy comes in the morning" (Psalm 30:5).

While sorrow over Nathan's absence isn't just something we *went* through, but in fact continue to *go* through, the Lord Himself continues to go with us through it. Still, life is not the same.

Other friends who have also known great sorrow expressed it this way after losing a son: "We now know terminal sadness. Always on the fringe of a laugh, there is a remembrance. And while we do not doubt that he's in the best place, we do so miss his face, and we will for the rest of our lives."

However, in the midst of the "missing," the Lord is with us and gives us His comfort at all times.

The Old Testament prophet Jeremiah mourned for his wayward nation and, at times, struggled to glimpse God in his grief. He prayed:

> O Hope of Israel,
> Its Savior in time of distress,
> Why are You like a stranger in the land
> Or like a traveler who has pitched his
>   tent for the night? (Jeremiah 14:8).

Even then, however, his soul came to rest in this blessed assurance: "Yet You are in our midst, O LORD" (Jeremiah 14:9).

God's presence with us in our grief is the one thing that can dispel the cold darkness. So, with the psalmist we say:

> But as for me, I will hope continually,
> And will praise You yet more and more
>   (Psalm 71:14).

From Glenda…Our Times

A time to love…
ECCLESIASTES 3:9

I was decorating the Christmas tree on a bright December day.

Before Nathan died, I always anticipated Christmas and enjoyed and participated in all the festivities that surround the Christmas season. Now, while we still do special things to celebrate the birth of Jesus, some of the superficial customs no longer merit the attention I used to give them. I still enjoy our Christmas tree, though, so I worked at it busily with Preston in the next room (we've found that distance while decorating helps keep us fond of each other!).

At one point, I stepped back to evaluate whether the tree was complete and decided it needed just a few more decorations. I slid my hand into the bottom of the bag of unused ornaments. I felt something larger than just an ornament and pulled it out of the bag. What appeared in my hand knocked the breath out of me. I just stood there, stared, and then called out to Preston. It was a stocking, and the name on the top was NATHAN.

Nathan's grandmother (my mother) had given him that stocking the first year of his life. I had lovingly filled it every Christmas Eve for him to open Christmas morning. One of my favorite times of year was shopping for stocking stuffers for Nathan—perhaps finding a reminder of a joke we had between the two of us or a gift tailored uniquely to him that was chosen to say, "I love you."

On this day, however—as much as I wanted to hang Nathan's stocking with all the other family members' stockings so I could fill it up for Christmas morning—I just had to stand there and hold it, empty.

Such a moment makes time stand still and grief roll in like a wave.

Even now, several years after Nathan went to heaven, those moments still happen. In talking with many others who have lost children and in hearing how things have gone in their lives afterward, I have accepted that these moments will probably happen for the rest of my life.

Holidays and family meal times are still the hardest. His birthday is a great hurdle. The first birthday we could not celebrate with him in person—about ten months after he fell—we still wanted his birthday to be a celebration (this is still the case). To make it a little easier, we spent the weekend together as a family at the Carolina coast.

As part of his celebration, we got the bright idea one night of having the first annual Nathan Parrish *Deal or No Deal* game. Perhaps you've watched the program on television. We all played. I was the host, as well as the girl who held the case containing the winning dollar amount. Preston was the banker—we even used real money (what were we thinking?).

Trust me, it ended up costing us some dollars, but it did help put a little fun and energy into a deeply difficult day. Believe it or not, after all our silliness, we still wept.

What a strange mixture of emotions!

As you come to your own difficult occasions, I'd encourage you to feel free to think outside the box. Going through the motions of your usual traditions may not be the best plan for you. In our family, we haven't been able to bring ourselves to do many of the same things in the same places as when Nathan was still with us. We have gravitated toward fresh scenery and new experiences while still facing the reality of what's changed in our lives.

Of course, everyone is different, and you will figure out what is best for you. Be affirmed, though, that it isn't dishonoring to approach the seasons a little differently than before. Just do what seems most helpful for you—even if others may not understand!

Nathan is not present with us anymore. The fact that he was such a vital part of our family's life makes us especially miss him when we are together. It is a pain that only the Comforter can soothe.

To help the disciples after Christ's departure, the Comforter came. So, it is in precisely such moments of need that we can rely on Him. Thank God for His promise, "As one whom his mother comforts, so I will comfort you" (Isaiah 66:13).

I know we will continue to experience challenging moments as we miss Nathan. We can mix up the routine as much as we want. We can go to new places and do new things. Truthfully, however, nothing can really take away the ache in our heart except asking God to comfort us.

Even as you continue to miss your loved one, I am praying that you will also know God's comfort on this road of grief.

I'm also praying that the hope of being in His presence will give you the courage to press on…at all times.

9

In Every Place

I FIRST SAW THE PLAY *Peter Pan* when I was in elementary school. Originally titled *Peter Pan: or, The Boy Who Wouldn't Grow Up*, Barrie's play debuted in London in 1904. I didn't know until recently that the background from which author J.M. Barrie penned it involved tragedy and grief.

A pivotal experience in Barrie's formative years was that his older brother David died in a skating accident at age 13. One writer characterized the death as "a catastrophe beyond belief" from which Barrie's mother "never fully recovered."[1] (I wonder what he meant by "fully recovered.") Some have suggested his mother may have drawn comfort from the idea that David, by dying at that young age, might ever remain a boy, and that this may have been Barrie's inspiration for the character Peter Pan.

I don't know whether this theory of Peter Pan's origin is true. I certainly don't find in Scripture the idea that when young people die, they remain in a perpetual state of earthly adolescence.

However, one aspect of Peter Pan's story intrigues me as I think about the comfort and hope God offers us in the course of our grief. It has to do with the idea of becoming separated from something that is ever present.

If you've seen it, you know that *Peter Pan* opens with Peter losing his shadow when he is detected eavesdropping by the bedroom window as the Darling children's mother reads them a bedtime story. When he returns to find and retrieve his shadow, daughter Wendy Darling sees him and helps to reattach it.

Peter's separation from his shadow—an experience that in real life would be ludicrous—brings to mind the experience of the Old Testament prophet Jonah. When Jonah didn't like what God was calling him to do, he attempted to flee from the presence of the Lord (Jonah 1:3). However, Jonah learned that, no matter where he was, it just wasn't possible for him to escape the presence of the Lord.

He discovered the truth of David's words in Psalm 139:7-8:

> Where can I go from Your Spirit?
> Or where can I flee from Your presence?
> If I ascend to heaven, You are there;
> If I make my bed in Sheol, behold, You are there.

The same is true for us in our times of grief. No place is beyond the reach of the God who loves us and who wants us to know His comfort and hope. This truth has been especially precious to us as we have found ourselves in some places we never would have chosen to be.

Late on the day before Nathan's funeral took place, Glenda and I drove to the cemetery where his body would soon be buried. Friends had located a plot for us that was available. Being familiar with the general area of the cemetery and not really having the time or emotional energy to do a lot of real estate shopping at that point, Glenda and I agreed to purchase it without laying eyes on the actual rectangle of sod where Nathan would be buried. Now, though, just hours before his interment, we wanted to see it before arriving there the next day with family and friends.

As we drove into the cemetery, we were mostly silent, sharing the emotions of the moment without talking. Winding our way along the cemetery's road, we came to the designated section and parked the car. It was late afternoon, and the sun was beginning to slip below the trees. Glenda and I got out of our respective sides of the car, the sound of our closing doors punctuating the chilly air. No one else was in sight. We walked hand in hand to the specific plot of ground now reserved for Nathan, passing the grave markers of others—some old, some young—whose bodies had been buried nearby.

I guess we really hadn't thought about it, but the usual "setting of the stage" for burial was not to take place until the next morning. What that meant was that when we got to Nathan's spot, there was no tent, no draping, no carpet, no flowers…nothing. The only thing there for our eyes to see was a weathered four-by-eight-foot piece of plywood laid by cemetery staff across a six-foot-deep hole in the ground.

That was it—a gaping hole, ready to receive the body of our beloved son.

The starkness of the sight gripped my gut. I almost wanted to throw up. Glenda and I couldn't really say much of anything. We just stood there, held each other close, breathed deeply, and sobbed…now and then casting a glance at that hole and trying to get past the disbelief that this was really happening to us.

In one sense, we were completely alone in that moment as the only two people on earth who fully knew the sorrow of our tragedy. But we were not alone—God was with us. He fully knew the sorrow we felt because His own Son was placed in a tomb after dying for our sins. He alone could comfort us, and He did, enabling us to go forward through the hours and days that lay ahead. He showed Himself faithful to us in that lonely place.

That hole in the ground in the cemetery is not the only place God has shown Himself strong for us in the days since Nathan died. A week or so later, we traveled to California to retrieve Nathan's belongings from the camp where he had been working. While there, Gregory and I, along with a friend, hiked some 2000 feet up the rugged mountain that Nathan had last hiked to see firsthand the place where he fell.

Because the recovery of his body had stretched into the night and darkness had combined with the terrain and elements to make the operation somewhat precarious, emergency workers had marked their trail by periodically taping trees as they ascended. That way, even in the dark they could see how to get down as they carried the stretcher bearing his body. When Gregory and I climbed that same trail just days afterward, the tape was still there—a witness to the grim events that had unfolded at that very spot.

For me, that trail became a trail of tears. As I hiked, I tried my best to grasp what had occurred, but it was hard. Most of all, I just wished Nathan were with us, talking and laughing and pointing out scenes of beauty as he had done on the many hikes he and Gregory and I had taken together over the years. After all, the view from up there really was spectacular, which was why he had enjoyed climbing to it. Now, though, he was seeing something unspeakably greater.

My point is simply this: the Lord really is present with us in every place—whether we're peering into a hole in the ground where the body of our loved one is about to be placed or gazing from a mountaintop at the last vista our loved one saw before entering eternity.

The Lord is also present with us in every place in between, to sustain and enable us to continue with life until we too get to heaven.

The assurance He gives us is that no place—absolutely no place—is a place where He will not be with us.

From Glenda…Our Times

A time to gather stones…
ECCLESIASTES 5:3

I stared out the small window as the plane flew through the clouds. Time had lost its meaning. It was the hardest day of my life—the day we traveled across the country from our home in North Carolina to retrieve Nathan's belongings.

Landing in Los Angeles, we rented a car and began the three-hour drive to the town where Nathan had been living when he died. We had not previously been to the camp where he worked. We passed through towns he had mentioned and saw sights he had described. We understood why he hated the Southern California traffic he would encounter as he left the airport and how glad he always was once he reached the picturesque, serene mountaintop where the camp was located.

As we headed into the rugged terrain of the San Jacinto mountain range, I identified with him on every mile of that ride. Cresting the top of the mountain, we witnessed the most amazing sunset I have ever seen. Nathan savored those sunsets, and watching this one was a gift to my heart.

We drove into the camp just as night was falling. The cold air and darkness perfectly set the scene for the mood I was in. The camp director, Allan, greeted us.

Allan had been Nathan's boss and almost immediately began sharing how much the camp team loved Nathan. As we entered the administration building, he pointed to a piece of paper on a bulletin board. It was a piece of paper that bore funny sayings, Bible verses, and encouraging words in Nathan's handwriting for the staff and anyone else who entered.

It was so hard at that moment for my brain to absorb what was happening. However, Allan kept reassuring us that Nathan had done what he set out to do: love and encourage everyone he met.

Then Allan walked us to the cabin where Nathan had been living. We entered, and he opened the door to Nathan's room.

I was paralyzed.

It smelled like Nathan.

As I looked around the room, everything I saw embodied him.

His keyboard, which he had taken back to camp with him after Christmas, was in the corner.

His clothes were there.

His books were there.

His climbing gear was there.

Everything that represented his life was there—only he was not.

I knelt and wept.

Allan left Preston and me alone. After spending some time there, I clutched Nathan's journal, and we left. We planned to return the next morning with Gregory to begin going through Nathan's belongings. However, at this moment, we felt heavy.

The air was heavy.

Life itself seemed heavy.

I wondered if I would ever feel any different.

Preston and I went to a local restaurant for dinner that night. As we entered the building, I spotted a newspaper stand outside the door with a picture on the front page of rescuers entering the forest to retrieve Nathan's body. I was numb.

The next morning, Allan invited us to his home for waffles with his precious family. Nathan admired Allan and his wife, Heidi, and their three boys (they've since added two more). Preston, Gregory, Gregory's friend Mike who was with us, and I so appreciated visiting with them.

Over breakfast, Allan and Heidi shared with us how much they enjoyed Nathan and were inspired and emboldened by his faith in Jesus. They also observed how Nathan was not afraid to be himself. It was then, sitting in a place I had never before been, that I realized God had answered this mother's prayers.

The psalmist wrote:

> But as for me, my prayer is to You, O Lord, at
> an acceptable time;
> O God, in the greatness of Your lovingkindness,
> Answer me with Your saving truth (Psalm 69:13).

Over the years, I have prayed for each of my children as they've left home that God would put His people in their path. There that day, I saw that God had done just that for Nathan, without me even knowing it. It was humbling to sense this family's heart, hear their testimony of faith, and learn how they had cared for my son.

Throughout the rest of that difficult day, we saw God's hand everywhere we turned. We met other people who knew Jesus and who loved Nathan and had been encouraged by him. For me, personally, God made it profoundly clear that He had known my mother's heart and heard every prayer I had prayed over my son's life.

Not only had He heard my prayers, He had answered them. In the middle of walking through this nightmare, there was God. His presence was not elusive but tangible. We could see Him at work. He visibly showed me that, while answers to our prayers may not come immediately, we can be assured He hears us and will answer in His perfect way and time.

I might never have known how God specifically answered my prayers had Nathan not gone to be with Him. God took the difficulty of that day and turned it into encouragement. He showed us beauty in the ashes.

That "showing" goes on—as I was writing these very words, we received a message from Allan on the latest anniversary of Nathan's death. He wrote:

> This week always brings thoughts about Nathan and prayers for your family. One of the amazing things about Nathan is how unaffected he was by the peer pressure to back off on his faith in Christ. It was obvious that through teaching and trial he had found his Savior. Sadly, most young Christians become more interested in fitting in with the group than focusing on Christ. This invariably leads to compromise. Not so with Nathan. As a matter of fact, due to his unconventional way of worshipping his God he tended to attract his peers' interest. He did things like beat his drum and burn sage smudges at his open-invitation Bible studies.

Allan went on to tell us yet another funny story about Nathan, which showed both his sincerity and his creativity:

> It was the sage smudging that got him into a little trouble one time. Another staff member reported smelling

marijuana smoke wafting out of his room. It is automatic in our company that if such an allegation is made the person in question is drug tested. Our drug tests are very comprehensive. We suddenly descend on the suspect and haul them off to be tested. If a person has been using any known drug we will find out. Nathan was very surprised but readily agreed to the test. He came through with flying colors. Not a trace of anything. Our little believer, Nathan, then went back to his life of uniquely worshipping his God AND in his own way fitting in with his peers.

Perhaps you are having the most difficult day of your life. If so, I want you to know that God is there.

Are you crying over a lost child or loved one? If you've cried out to Jesus for him or her, He has heard you. The fact that your loved one may not be on earth any longer does not mean that He did not hear you or does not care. In this journey of grief, we must cling to what we know, not just what we feel.

I pray that you will see God as you walk through these days, and that He will comfort and encourage your heart in wonderfully unexpected ways. He has done that for me.

10

In Every Outward Circumstance

IN MY EXPERIENCE, the people who say the most profound things are not necessarily those who spend most of their time in the glare of the spotlight, whether in show business, sports, business, politics, or even religion.

Rather, they are often people whom the world does not know, people who have suffered a great deal, and who by clinging to God in their suffering have gained a perspective that can't be staged or "spun." A similar observation came from German pastor Dietrich Bonhoeffer, who at 39 years of age was put to death for his resistance against Adolph Hitler during World War II.

Imprisoned by Hitler's minions for more than 18 months before his death, Bonhoeffer wrote extensively during that time. Some of his writings were published after his execution as *Letters and Papers from Prison.* There, he said: "We must form our estimate of men less from their achievements and failures, and more from their sufferings."[1]

FINDING HOPE IN TIMES OF GRIEF

The writer of the book of Ecclesiastes expresses this same thought:

> It is better to go to a house of mourning
> Than to go to a house of feasting,
> Because that is the end of every man,
> And the living takes it to heart.
> Sorrow is better than laughter,
> For when a face is sad a heart may be happy.
> The mind of the wise is in the house of mourning,
> While the mind of fools is in the house of pleasure
> (Ecclesiastes 7:2-4).

It really can be true that "the mind of the wise is in the house of mourning." For those passing through grief, the fact is that their mourning is often the result of not only one devastating event but of several that happen simultaneously or in rapid succession. In my interaction with hurting people, as well as in our own lives, we've seen that multiple layers of difficulty and loss frequently precede and/or follow the "big one" that hits them.

This was true for Job. After the initial blows that hit Job—the loss of his wealth and the deaths of his ten children—he lost his health. However, that wasn't the end of his woes. His response to his "friends," in chapter 19 of the Bible book bearing his name, gives us a glimpse of the additional losses and conflicts he experienced:

> How long will you torment me
> And crush me with words?
> These ten times you have insulted me;
> You are not ashamed to wrong me.
> Even if I have truly erred,

My error lodges with me.
Behold, I cry, "Violence!" but I get no answer;
I shout for help, but there is no justice.
He has walled up my way so that I cannot pass,
And He has put darkness on my paths.

He has stripped my honor from me
And removed the crown from my head.
He breaks me down on every side, and I am gone;
And He has uprooted my hope like a tree.
He has removed my brothers far from me,
And my acquaintances are completely estranged
    from me.
My relatives have failed,
And my intimate friends have forgotten me.
Those who live in my house and my maids
    consider me a stranger.
I am a foreigner in their sight.
I call to my servant, but he does not answer;
I have to implore him with my mouth.
My breath is offensive to my wife,
And I am loathsome to my own brothers.
Even young children despise me;
I rise up and they speak against me.
All my associates abhor me,
And those I love have turned against me.

Can you hear his compounded pain? I can. In addition to the
initial calamities that befell him, Job also had to deal with misun-
derstanding, accusations, slander, insults, injustice, dishonor, in-
subordination, estrangement, and betrayal—all while having been

reduced to poverty, feeling physically horrible, and grieving his heart out! Can you imagine?

When we go through even a small measure of such calamity, the wave-upon-wave of tragedy that hits us can leave us asking, "Did I do something, or fail to do something, that caused this?"

If our own proneness to second-guessing, regret, and guilt isn't enough, other people sometimes say things to us that raise and re-inforce such questioning. After Nathan died, someone said to me, "When I heard of your son's death, I prayed and asked God to take out of my life anything that would cause one of my own children to be taken."

Perhaps it was unintended, but there seemed to be an assumption behind that statement that there had indeed been something in *my* life that *caused* Nathan to be taken. Thankfully, Scripture shows us that, when tragedy strikes, this isn't necessarily the case.

Job said:

> My face is flushed from weeping,
> And deep darkness is on my eyelids,
> Although there is no violence in my hands,
> And my prayer is pure (Job 16:16-17).

One day Jesus and His disciples passed a man who had been blind since birth. The disciples asked Him, "Rabbi, who sinned, this man or his parents, that he was born blind?"

Jesus answered, "It was neither that this man sinned, nor his parents; but it was so that the works of God might be displayed in him" (John 9:3).

The fact is, we live in a world that is out of order. Things happen over which we have no control. The writer of Ecclesiastes makes this point by observing, "If the clouds are full, they pour out rain upon the earth; and whether a tree falls toward the south or toward the north, wherever the tree falls, there it lies" (Ecclesiastes 11:3).

Scripture also clues us in to the fact that, sometimes, "the righteous are taken away to be spared from evil" (Isaiah 57:1 NIV). We believe this may have been the case for Nathan.

Whatever happens in our lives, God is God…He is faithful… and He is great enough to use even the unspeakably difficult events in our lives for His glory and for our good.

So, even if the great tragedy before you right now is compounded by other difficulties, take heart…look up…He is with you and has not forsaken you.

Know, though, that others may not always be with you. We thank God for the faithful friends who have walked with us in our grief. They have blessed us with kindness upon kindness. We will be forever grateful. But be aware that when you're months down the road from your catastrophic event, most people will no longer "get" that your tragedy is a continuing factor in everything you do and are. For them, life has moved on and, while they certainly recall this event in your life, they are oblivious to the large presence and force that remains in the middle of your heart and soul.

This can mean they are unsure about how to understand, interpret, or respond to some of the things you say and do, and they may expect you to deal with subjects you don't have the least interest in addressing. It may also mean that some people see your weakness and vulnerability as an opportunity to advance their own personal agendas.

Clinging to Christ will keep you from succumbing to what would be yet another tragedy for you: developing a root of bitterness in your heart. Don't let this happen—it will immerse you even deeper in pain, and it's not worth it.

An oft-repeated statement, uttered by people in all sorts of circumstances, is "I wish I had known then what I know now." When it comes to grief, and to relating to others who are in the midst of it, that's the way I feel. Because of our own experience, I now understand at least a little more of what's involved. Many times over the years, however, I'm sure I responded to people living with sorrow in ways that were inconsiderate and unhelpful.

For example, my paternal grandparents—now deceased—lived through the deaths of two of their adult children in a span of seven years or so. I never met either this uncle, who was my father's older and only brother and who died in the military, or this aunt, who suffered from a congenital heart defect. Over the years, I was oblivious to how this must have affected them. I now know, however, that their deaths were no doubt an ever-present part of my grandparents' life during all the years I knew them.

Thankfully, the death of a loved one who trusts in Christ isn't the end of life. As Dietrich Bonhoeffer was led naked to his hanging, the hope of Christ enabled him to declare, "This is the end—for me the beginning of life."[2]

The camp doctor witnessing the event wrote, "At the place of execution, he again said a short prayer and then climbed the few steps to the gallows, brave and composed. His death ensued after a few seconds. In the almost fifty years that I worked as a doctor, I have hardly ever seen a man die so entirely submissive to the will of God."[3]

May God help us, whatever our outward circumstances may be, to be filled with the hope of Christ, and to completely trust our loving heavenly Father.

From Glenda…Our Times

A time to embrace…

ECCLESIASTES 3:5

The day before Nathan died, if you had asked me to name my friends, I would have handed you a long list.

If you had asked me the same question a year after Nathan went to heaven, I would have handed you a shorter list, but the names on that paper would have represented people with whom I know I have a proven, solid friendship. I would have also told you that I've learned I need to be a better friend.

The dictionary defines a friend as "a person with whom one is allied in a struggle or cause; a comrade. One who supports, sympathizes with, or patronizes a group, cause, or movement."

I am humbled by those individuals who have given the word *friendship* authentic meaning in my life. They are people who have supported, sympathized, and persevered with our family through this struggle of monumental proportion.

They have tried hard to understand what walking in our shoes involves and to help us keep moving forward.

They have filled in blanks amidst the daily routine of life when we could not even see the blanks that needed to be filled.

For example, one of the early blanks that had to be filled—but that was beyond me at the time—was helping JesseRuth get ready for a dance scheduled just days after Nathan's death. My friends saw the need and acted, taking JesseRuth shopping for shoes, a dress, and a pocketbook. They had her nails done. They made the event what it needed to be for her—fun. I will be forever grateful for their foresight and ability to see those practical needs that were way beyond my ability to handle in the days immediately following Nathan's death.

Preston and I looked at each other many times during the first year or two after Nathan died and said, "Why would anyone want to be with us?" We were not spontaneous, encouraging, or fun. We tried to be, but our attempts were futile. We just plain hurt too much, and simply functioning took everything we had. I felt as though I were walking around with a continuous flu.

"Harsh" and "awful" are apt ways to describe the reality of feeling "left behind." Dealing with these conditions involves a much longer time frame than anyone who hasn't experienced them can imagine—longer than I would have ever thought.

The Bible, however, says, "A friend loves at all times, and a brother is born for adversity" (Proverbs 17:17). We experienced the truth of this passage through people who stuck with us. Among them were my own brothers.

The night Nathan died, one of Preston's first calls was to my brother Greg. He asked him to notify my parents in person of Nathan's death. Doing so required Greg and my youngest brother, Todd, to drive in the middle of the night to a town four hours away to give my parents this devastating message. We knew we could count on them because they loved Nathan and were the best ones to break the news to my parents, who had also invested much into Nathan's life. Brothers are indeed born for the day of adversity.

Christian brothers and sisters are no exception. A brother or sister in Christ who is also your true friend is a valued treasure.

Loving someone in the midst of grief can challenge the best of friendships because, for a time, there is often not a lot of mutuality in the friendship equation. The grieving person's needs are too great.

In such a situation, you quickly learn who the friends are that love you regardless of whether you can contribute anything to the relationship. It humbles me every time I think about the friends who have loved me "at all times."

I'm sure it wasn't easy. I realize that I was a great frustration to many people in the first year after Nathan's death. For the most part, I needed to be by myself and spend time praying and processing what had happened. Family members and friends would reach out to me, and I just could not respond. Some stopped trying, and I don't blame them. Others persevered until I was able and ready to respond. I am grateful for both but amazed at the ones who persevered.

In reflecting on my experience, I have had to ask myself, "Glenda, what kind of friend are you?"

I am not sure I like the answer because I know I have room for improvement. These days, I find myself asking God to show me opportunities and ways to demonstrate friendship to others, and to give me the necessary love and patience for people with deep needs.

Recently, I was talking to a friend whose own son had died eight years earlier. She said, "I lost many friends as I grieved because it was just too difficult for them."

However, other people walking through grief can testify to the fact that *all* their friends stuck with them. Praise God!

My own experience has been that it was just too hard for some people, and they moved on with their own lives. Believe me, we understand.

I want to be a friend that loves at all times, especially when someone is in a hard, dark place. Friends and family who have persevered with me have painted me a clear picture of what true friendship is. And ultimately, the Lord has proved that He is the perfect friend, "who sticks closer than a brother" (Proverbs 18:24).

11

In Every Inner Condition

Have you ever wondered how some people can go through some of the worst tragedies imaginable, yet still have about them a strength, peace, and joy that are almost tangible?

I've known a few such people and have marveled over the way they endure tough circumstances and hard times while seldom if ever succumbing to frustration, anger, self-pity, or despair. To the contrary, they effuse hope—hope that has encouraged and blessed me in my own journey through life, and in my own times of grief.

In observing them and in reading the Scriptures, I've come to a conclusion: it really is a matter of a person's inner condition.

No matter what has happened in their outward circumstances, these people have clung to Christ inwardly, and that clinging— that moment-by-moment faith—has buoyed them above the events around them.

By contrast, when we aren't experiencing Him inwardly—in our spirits—even relatively mild difficulties can drag us down and swamp us with discouragement. As the old saying goes, "It's not the water outside the boat that sinks it—it's the water inside." This principle is found in the Bible.

Proverbs 18:14 says:

> The spirit of a man can endure his sickness,
> But as for a broken spirit who can bear it?

In his sorrow, Job said:

> My spirit is broken, my days are extinguished,
> The grave is ready for me (Job 17:1).

Now, it's worth noting that there is a time for "a broken spirit"—namely, when we come to God in repentance for our sins. King David knew this and wrote:

> The sacrifices of God are a broken spirit;
> A broken and a contrite heart, O God, You
>   will not despise (Psalm 51:17).

But when it comes to going through the trials of life, God wants to give us strong hearts that will see us through the difficult days. Psalm 34:18 says:

> The LORD is near to the brokenhearted
> And saves those who are crushed in spirit.

The Lord Jesus Himself said, "Blessed are those who mourn, for they shall be comforted" (Matthew 5:4).

British writer Samuel Johnson once said, "Hope is necessary in every condition. The miseries of poverty, of sickness, or captivity, would, without this comfort, be insupportable."[1] (He went on to assert that hope is necessary in times of prosperity as well.)

Experiencing the hope God offers us is the key to making it through grief and not becoming mired in depression. These two conditions—grief and depression—do, after all, involve similar symptoms.

According to mental health experts, symptoms of clinical depression can include:

- persistent sad, anxious, or "empty" feelings
- feelings of hopelessness and pessimism
- a sense of irritability, restlessness, or being slowed down
- fatigue or loss of energy
- feelings of worthlessness or guilt
- overeating or appetite loss
- difficulty concentrating, remembering details, and making decisions
- insomnia or excessive sleeping
- loss of interest in activities or hobbies once considered pleasurable
- recurring thoughts of death or suicide

When a number of these symptoms characterize a person regularly and for a sustained period, it may well indicate that a person is suffering clinical depression that calls for medical treatment. Significantly, however, *if these symptoms occur within two months of the loss of a loved one, they will not generally be diagnosed as depression!* Rather, they are viewed as an expected part of grief.[2]

Many of these "grief notes" can be heard in the cries of people in the Bible. Consider David's lament in Psalm 31:

> Be gracious to me, O Lord, for I am in distress; my eye
> is wasted away from grief, my soul and my body also
> (Psalm 31:9).

I can almost feel the physical effects of David's grief. The same is true in Psalm 38, also written by David:

> My loins are filled with burning,
> And there is no soundness in my flesh.
> I am benumbed and badly crushed;
> I groan because of the agitation of my heart.
> Lord, all my desire is before You;
> And my sighing is not hidden from You
>   (Psalm 38:7-9).

Note in this psalm David's reference to "agitation." Irritability—in fact, anger—often accompanies grief. Some people direct their anger toward God, blaming Him because He could have prevented their sorrow but did not do so. That's shortsighted. In Christ, God has shown us that He is ever good, wise, and faithful. Moreover, as someone once said, "The alternative to disappointment *with* God is disappointment *without* God, and that's far worse."

Sometimes, a grieving person's anger isn't directed toward God—it's just a general frustration over having to live with loss and pain, perhaps somewhat like a wounded animal that's surly. That's completely understandable. To whatever extent anger may have been part of my response to Nathan's death, that's probably the reason. However, trusting and resting in God's sovereign love and purposes is the remedy for it. Still, though, grief hurts.

In Psalm 137, the writer expressed the anguished cry of the Jews held captive in Babylon, in exile from their beloved homeland:

By the rivers of Babylon,
There we sat down and wept,
When we remembered Zion (Psalm 137:1).

Have you ever just "sat down and wept" upon the remembrance of someone you lost? We have, and not always in the most "convenient" places.

A year or so after Nathan died, I was sitting on an airplane. Without any apparent trigger from my surroundings, memories of Nathan began flooding my mind. In a minute or two, tears were flooding down my face. Somewhat self-conscious about melting down while surrounded by other passengers, I put on my sunglasses and buried my face in a magazine. Before long I felt God's comfort, and that release of emotion was probably therapeutic—I just wouldn't have chosen to do it in Seat 3C!

(By the way, we never know what struggle the person beside us on a plane or bus or train or in the checkout line at the store may be having.)

The apostle Paul mourned the lostness of his native people, Israel, who had rejected their Messiah. He wrote, "I have great sorrow and unceasing grief in my heart" (Romans 9:2).

The fact that the great apostle lived with sorrow and grief affords me some consolation. It is also a reminder that the greatest loss anyone can ever suffer is separation from God for eternity through rejection of His Son.

Making it possible for us to be reconciled to God rather than separated from Him is exactly the purpose for which Christ came, and for which He suffered grief: "In the days of His flesh, He offered up both prayers and supplications with loud crying and tears to the One able to save Him from death, and He was heard because of His piety" (Hebrews 5:9).

It's staggering to think that the earthly life and ministry of the Son of God Himself was marked by "loud crying and tears"—but it was. Jesus even wept at the tomb of His friend Lazarus (John 11:35). That makes the promise of His presence with us in our own times of inner sorrow all the more precious, and all the more comforting.

He says, "I will never desert you, nor will I ever forsake you" (Hebrews 13:5). Included in "never" and "ever" are all our moments of inner turmoil. Not one of them can ever be outside the reach of His everlasting arms.

Because He is always with us, even in our most desperate inner condition, His hope is always within reach…even for you, and even now.

From Glenda…Our Times

A time to sew together…
ECCLESIASTES 3:7

Grief is lonely. Each heart knows its own grief.

Understandably, many who come to your aid in the aftermath of tragedy will return to the busyness of their own lives. It seems as though life as they know it continues full speed while life as you know it will never be the same.

In addition, you may feel the weight of the general expectation just to "get over" your sadness. But what you are going through is unique to you and your family. Just like going through a wedding or birth, every little detail of your experience with the death of your loved one is personal to you.

Already I've mentioned that, in the immediate days after Nathan's death, I would sit for hours and nurse thoughts of him while trying to process how in this world I would be able to move forward without him here in our family equation. Even though I would pray, read Scripture, and try to talk to people, I felt stuck in a pit of the worst sorrow imaginable. Thankfully, worshipping the Lord, particularly through music, gave me perspective and strength.

The day before Nathan's funeral, I dissolved into our living room couch and listened to a CD by our good friend, songwriter and musician Anne Barbour.[3] Scripture speaks of a joyful heart being good medicine (Proverbs 17:22). That day, Anne unknowingly helped me rejoice in the Lord, even in the midst of my grief, and it was medicine to me. Her anointed lyrics gave me strength to get through the rest of that day.

For a while after Nathan died, worshipping God through music was a spiritual lifeline for me. When you cannot concentrate enough even to hold a complete thought or read something and comprehend it, music is an easy way to lift your spirit and mind toward God. It was through the music played and sung at Nathan's funeral that the power of the Holy Spirit came upon me, enabling me to stand to my feet with my hands in the air to worship a heavenly Father whose plans are greater than my own.

After the funeral, sorrow quickly turned into loneliness. Loneliness comes over you in the most unexpected ways. I found myself going through a process of wanting to rid my life of anything superficial and concentrate on what seemed truly important. This process probably seemed peculiar to onlookers (including my family).

For example, I've always enjoyed jewelry and accessories—I had no desire to wear any.

I previously loved getting my nails done—I quit having them done.

The things I once found hilarious now did not even make me crack a smile.

I am sure it was hard to be around me during this time, and I'm thankful for those who tolerated me.

Even though Preston and I were walking through this grief together—still, I was lonely.

Lonely…period.

I was in a land where I had never been, and I felt like a lone castaway. As I called out to God to get me through these days, the words of the psalmist meant so much: "Turn to me and be gracious to me, for I am lonely and afflicted" (Psalm 25:16).

God did turn to me, and He did help me in my loneliness and affliction. I prayed that He would show me the things that He wanted me to see in those days of sorrow. Soon I started writing down what He showed me. What you are reading on these pages is some of what He showed me.

It has taken me some time to get to the place where I am able to share these thoughts. I am praying that, as you are reading them, you will turn to Him and feel His graciousness in the midst of your own loneliness and affliction.

He is a gracious God…He has been gracious to me…He will be gracious to you.

It is important that we not think of ourselves as abnormal if the loneliness of grief seems prolonged and never ending. In my experience, grief has felt at times like slogging through life with concrete blocks tied to my feet.

In grief, your mind will process things more slowly.

All the while, your heart will continue to ache.

In Every Inner Condition

Do not be mistaken. Operating under these conditions does *not* mean you are not experiencing the grace of God. His grace is what enables you to get out of bed in the morning without throwing up. Even if you do throw up, He will help you to keep functioning.

Though I am now walking through days that feel more normal, the loneliness has not completely gone away. Sometimes it still feels as if people don't respond to me in the same way they once did. I admit that at times I feel myself overcompensating to prove I am still normal—the same me as before, even though so much has changed.

It still feels lonely when I walk into a room and have the sense that people are avoiding me because there is a level of discomfort in knowing what to say to me.

It is lonely when you are carrying on with a seemingly normal activity and grief sweeps over you without a trace of warning.

Jesus, however, also knew loneliness. The Bible says that Jesus went to a lonely place to pray (Luke 5:16 NIV).

He went to lonely places to stay when He could not minister in towns (Mark 1:45 NIV).

My experience with the loneliness of grief has provided me with a better understanding of the loneliness of our Lord as He walked this earth.

And His most intense loneliness—infinitely greater than any we will ever know—was in the awful darkness He experienced on the cross, when He bore our sins (Matthew 27:46).

Praise God that we can call out to Him in our loneliness.

Praise Him that He has walked in our shoes and understands our cries.

Praise Him for responding to our despair with His gracious love.

12

In Every Season of Life

Do you know what I find sobering? The fact that I can now look back over my life and assess it not just year by year, but decade by decade.

There was a time when the nine months of a school year seemed like forever (I'm sure some of the teachers who had the misfortune of having me in their classes felt the same way!)

Now, though, I understand more and more what Moses meant when he wrote:

> As for the days of our life, they contain seventy years,
> Or if due to strength, eighty years...
> For soon it is gone and we fly away (Psalm 90:10).

Moses actually lived to be 120. Some people live longer than the norm that he observed, and others live less. Daddy's time on this earth came to a close in his eightieth year, precisely within the time frame that Moses noted. Nathan "flew away"—or, as someone expressed it, "fell into heaven"—in his twenty-sixth year. Both seemed "soon."

The contrast in their ages underscores the truth that "man does not know his time" (Ecclesiastes 9:12). It also urges us to make sure that we ourselves are walking with God today—now—because we do not know how many tomorrows we have.

At this stage in life, my orientation is twofold. On the one hand, my eyes are ultimately fixed on the "prize of the upward call of God in Christ Jesus" (Philippians 4:13). At the same time, however, I'm mindful of Christ's admonition not to "worry about tomorrow; for tomorrow will care for itself" (Matthew 6:34).

In other words, it's important to be diligent in following Christ moment by moment, day by day, and in seizing opportunities to know Him better and to make Him known, as they arise. Then one day, as we follow Him step-by-step, we'll get to step into heaven. Hallelujah!

Even in living with this orientation, though, I sometimes find myself looking back. As I do, I give thanks for God's graciousness in the past, and I seek to learn from His dealings with me. I reflect on His presence with us in every season of life, in all of the events that each one has held.

For example, as I look back to the time when I was about 25 years old, I thank Him for the unbridled passion and energy He gave me for any and every task—especially ministry-related ones—no matter how large or small. I also shudder to think of what some of the consequences might have been had He not protected me from my naïveté.

As I look back to the time when I was about 35 years old, I thank Him for the desire He put in me to go deeper in my knowledge of Him through the Scriptures, and to help others do the same. I'm also embarrassed by some of the brash presumption I recall that no doubt caused others to wonder whether I was really worth their investment of effort and resources.

As I look back to the time when I was about 45 years old, I thank Him for the understanding He gave me of His purposes throughout history, and how this lifetime was my opportunity to be a link in this generation toward "the summing up of all things in Christ, things in the heavens and things on the earth" (Ephesians 1:10). It was also at that time I began to realize the sand was slipping surely and steadily from the hourglass of my own time here on this earth. I became even more aware of the importance of treating people right and of my own need to continue growing in this area.

I'll stop there with reciting the decades! Suffice it to say, though, that these days my prayer is to be able one day to say with the apostle Paul, "I have fought the good fight, I have finished the course, I have kept the faith" (2 Timothy 4:7). Most days, I feel I still have a long way to go.

However, through all these days—through all the seasons of life—God has been with us and has given us everything we needed for each particular moment.

Glenda and I have now lived through the births of four children (not to mention their childhood and adolescence)…the weddings of two…the funeral of one, within a week of the funeral of my father… the births of several spanking-new grandbabies…and lots of other "stuff" before, after, and in-between. The presence and help of the true and living God has been the one constant in all these things.

With His presence, we have experienced the promise that Scripture gives to those who seek to please God and who delight in His Word:

> He will be like a tree firmly planted
>   by streams of water,
> Which yields its fruit in its season
> And its leaf does not wither (Psalm 1:3).

We have experienced, even in our times of grief, the promise of Jesus: "If anyone is thirsty, let him come to Me and drink. He who believes in Me, as the Scripture said, 'From his innermost being will flow rivers of living water'" (John 7:37-38).

In our present trials, and as we look at whatever life may hold in the days ahead, we have come to the faith-founded, experience-proven conviction that Christ is our hope, and that this hope "does not disappoint, because the love of God has been poured out within our hearts through the Holy Spirit who was given to us" (Romans 5:5).

I say all this to encourage you forward in your journey, especially in your time of grief. While your present sorrow may well be beyond your capacity to handle, it is not beyond God's capacity. Jesus said, "The things that are impossible with people are possible with God" (Luke 18:27).

We've found His words to be true and have seen that, even when we have felt utterly exhausted and depleted emotionally, physically, and even spiritually, the life He puts in us by His Spirit "does not wither."

We're praying that you too will discover His sufficiency and reliability…in this and in every other season of your life.

From Glenda…Our Times

A time to speak…
ECCLESIASTES 3:8

Nathan had a vibrant relationship with Christ when he died, but there had been years when he wandered in "the far country." Two letters, written five years apart, strikingly illustrate his journey.

The first letter is one that Preston wrote Nathan when he was not walking with the Lord and we both were deeply concerned about him. Nathan had been home from college for the weekend, and during his visit, we saw indications he was making choices that took him away from, rather than closer to, the Lord. After talking and praying for discernment, Preston put into writing a loving but clear message that we felt he desperately needed at that moment. In part it read:

> Nathan, for some time I have been thinking about your present situation in life and I think it is timely for me to express my thoughts to you. My first thought is of the fact that, since before you were born, you have been God's gift to us, for whom we have always been thankful. Closely related is the truth that God has built into you enormous potential for good and that your life can be an amazing demonstration of His love, grace, and power to many other people. Mom and I pray continuously that this will come to pass. While we don't know—and it is not our role to say—what specific shape this might take, we are convinced that He has given you life for this purpose.
>
> These convictions about you are precisely why your present state of being is of such concern to us. Clearly, you have chosen to pursue a course that, if unchanged, will cause you and others irreparable damage and sorrow and that will lead to forfeiture of many of the blessings God wants to bestow upon you. This is evident in a number of areas, including your ongoing resistance to the lordship of Jesus Christ in your life.
>
> Nathan, while you and everyone else will have spiritual questions, I don't believe that you have any

crippling perplexity about Christian living. You know the truth—you just are opting not to act on it. That is a very dangerous course, which causes you, us, and God Himself great sorrow. Worst of all, if you persist in this course, the consequences will only grow more grim.

It is time, Nathan, for you to choose for or against the lordship of Christ in your life. Never will there be a better or easier time than now. And as you know, not to decide is to decide.

Know that I stand ready to encourage and help you in any way I can in experiencing God's best for your life. And know that if you choose to continue living out of fellowship with Him, both love for you and grief over your decision and its unfolding consequences will fill Mom's and my hearts continually.

Love always,
Dad

The impact of Nathan's wandering on my life was significant. I loved Nathan with all my heart and soul. He was my son. His wandering caused me many anxious moments. I talked with him for hours on end about the decisions he was making, hoping it would change his mind and his direction. I lay awake many nights thinking of him and praying for him.

But—praise God—the story did not end there. Our prodigal finally did come to his senses and return home to the Lord. In the days that followed his death, we received many letters and confirmations of Nathan's deep commitment to the Lord. It became clear that the Lord used him and his witness to change the lives of others. Knowing he died in fellowship with Christ has brought me great comfort.

In addition to impacting many people outside our family for the Lord, Nathan also made a mark for Him within our family. This was demonstrated by a letter he wrote his younger sister five years after Preston's letter to him. Nathan's letter surfaced at an especially important moment a couple of years after he died.

One night, JesseRuth went to bed and then began missing Nathan greatly. She was just eleven when he died so naturally some of her grief set in more gradually than it did for the rest of the family. Nathan left for college when JesseRuth was five, and many of her memories are from his visits home or when we would go to see him. This particular night she was stricken to tears that she could not remember his voice. I asked her if she wanted to hear it (I have it on video) but that just seemed too hard for her at the moment.

We prayed. As we did so, I remembered that, as I had cleaned out her drawers, I had found a handwritten note from Nathan to her. Through tears, I read it to her. She cried too, but it comforted her. It comforted me because it reinforced the fact that, though Nathan had wandered, he had landed on solid ground in his relationship with Jesus Christ.

He wrote:

> I enjoyed spending some time with you when home on the weekends this past spring semester. Old Maids and cookies, Scrabble, coming to your swim meets, your birthday, New Year's with you and Hannah, and…well, it's just been great.
>
> I can see you already having a great fifth grade year, and I hope to be a part of it. The way that you're growing, it's fifth grade going on college. Love every minute of it.
>
> One thing that I really admire about you is your

heart for God. Keep remembering the Scriptures that you have memorized and read more. IF THERE IS ANYTHING YOU CAN LEARN FROM ME it is to STAY CLOSE TO THE LORD. Your life will be much better.

It's easy to get distracted sometimes, especially when you're in the middle of growing up. Remember Him in all that you do, and you will be greatly blessed even more than you may realize at that time.

I know that you have a few years before you become a teenager but keep these things in mind because they will still help you. Enough of this running on…

I love you,
Nathan

(Man, it is hard to sit here and look at his handwriting and type out these words, but maybe they will encourage you or someone you know.)

Nathan finally came to the point that he was tired of wandering and felt a real urgency to come back into the arms of Jesus. After that, he wanted everyone else he encountered to have that same urgency in their own heart and life. He knew firsthand that "now is *the acceptable time,*' behold, now is *'the day of salvation'*" (2 Corinthians 6:2, emphasis mine).

If you are struggling to have hope and to maintain a firm footing through the loss of someone dear to you, I pray that God's Word and His faithfulness in rescuing Nathan will help rekindle your faith in Jesus, and that you will draw close unto Him. He will walk with you and give you the direction you need in these hard times, and always.

PART 5

More Comfort:
We Are with Christ

In the well-known story of the Prodigal Son, Jesus presented God as a loving father who, even when his son left home to waste his life in a far country, still longed for him.

When he saw his son returning home, he ran to welcome him "while he was still a long way off" (Luke 15:20) and ordered a celebration, declaring that his son was dead but had come to life again (Luke 15:24).

It's crucial for us not to miss the main point Christ was making in this beloved story—namely, that God the Father longs for us to turn from our sins and come home to Him. When we make the decision to do so, He welcomes us with open arms, and all of heaven rejoices.

We hope by now you've "come home" to Him by placing your trust in Christ for forgiveness and eternal life. If you haven't yet, please don't put it off any longer. He loves you and wants you to know the comfort of His love and the embrace of His everlasting arms. Taking this step will make all the difference for you—now in your sorrow, and for eternity.

In thinking about finding hope in times of grief, though, let's not miss something else in the story: The father described his son as having been "dead." That says that he must have experienced many long days and nights of grief during his son's absence.

Notice also the response of this father to his "dead" son. Though physically separated from him, the son was never far from his mind and heart. (That's no doubt why he ran to him the moment he caught a glimpse of him!)

He ached to see him…to hear him…to hold him.

That sounds a lot like what grief has involved for us. Probably this is true for you too.

If so, you can find hope in knowing that our heavenly Father understands how we feel and has compassion for us as we grieve.

Already, we've discussed ways that He is present with us in our grief.

It's also wondrously true that, in our grief, we are ever present with Him…

13

In His Mind

I MENTIONED EARLIER that Nathan relished being able to watch the stars overhead as he fell asleep.

Do you know how many stars there are?

Without the aid of a telescope, roughly 3000 stars are visible in the nighttime sky of our hemisphere. Nathan loved looking at the myriad lights in the heavens from high in the mountains where he worked.

Astronomers estimate that our own galaxy, the Milky Way, may contain 200 *billion* stars. That's a lot of stars, huh?

But guess what—there are other galaxies. Some galaxies are believed to contain anywhere from a *trillion* to as many as ten *trillion* stars. And then…there may be as many as a trillion galaxies!

It's hard to comprehend such large numbers—whether of stars, people, or anything else. God does, though, and this matters greatly for people—for us—in grief.

Currently, the population of the world is heading toward seven billion people. In ten years or so, it may surpass eight billion. Yet when I fly into a vast metropolitan area like New York or Mexico

City—neither of which has more than about 20 *million* people—it boggles my mind just to look down upon the vast multitudes of people living there. I can't even begin to fathom the concerns and issues of each individual person. God, however, knows not only each star above but also each individual person below, in every house and room.

He not only sees each one in his or her personal circumstances, He knows exactly what's in their minds and hearts, and He wants to save and help them. As Psalm 147 says:

> He heals the brokenhearted
> And binds up their wounds.
> He counts the number of the stars;
> He gives names to all of them.
> Great is our Lord and abundant in strength;
> His understanding is infinite (Psalm 147:3-5).

It can be easy in grief to wonder whether *you* really matter to God. The answer is, *absolutely!* It's crucial for us to realize that neither God's understanding nor His strength is eclipsed by the severity of our sorrow.

The prophet Isaiah reflected on God's knowledge of the stars and declared:

> Lift up your eyes on high
> And see who has created these stars,
> The One who leads forth their host by number,
> He calls them all by name;
> Because of the greatness of His might and the
>   strength of His power,
> Not one of them is missing (Isaiah 40:26).

He then said that the God who keeps up with all the stars is also great enough to keep up with us:

> Do you not know? Have you not heard?
> The Everlasting God, the LORD, the Creator
>   of the ends of the earth
> Does not become weary or tired
> His understanding is inscrutable.
> He gives strength to the weary,
> And to him who lacks might He increases
>   power (Isaiah 40:27).

And he recorded this ageless promise of God's desire to hold us up:

> Though youths grow weary and tired,
> And vigorous young men stumble badly,
> Yet those who wait for the LORD
> Will gain new strength;
> They will mount up with wings like eagles,
> They will run and not get tired,
> They will walk and not become weary
>   (Isaiah 40:28-31).

Weary...tired...stumbling—we've been all of those things in our grief. Probably you have too. But God has not left us there, nor will He leave you there. Though you may feel like one obscure person among thousands, millions, or billions, let these truths be imprinted on your mind right now:

> He sees you...
> He knows you...

He understands your pain…

He offers you His comfort and hope…

You are ever in His mind.

Have you ever noticed that, when we truly love someone, he or she never really leaves our minds?

That's been Glenda's and my experience with our children and with each other. We think of each other early in the morning when only one of us has gotten out of bed (usually me!). We think of each other during the day, as we go about our respective activities. We think of each other when one of us wakes up in the middle of the night and the other continues snoring (again, usually me!).

We think of each other—and pray for each other—incessantly. After decades of marriage, I can say that this is the case even when we're irritating each other. In fact, I'm sure Glenda would say there have been times when she wished she didn't have to think of me!

Certainly there are moments when the task at hand is at the forefront of our thoughts. Always, though, whether in the middle of a task or immediately upon its completion, our thoughts return to each other. If we're physically separated, whether across town or across the globe, we're phoning, emailing, or texting as soon as possible to catch up on what's been happening and to make plans for the time we again come together.

This tendency we all have to bear our loved ones continually in mind is part of what makes dealing with their death so hard. We become so accustomed to enjoying a person's presence in our life and, when we're not actually with him or her, to anticipating it and reflecting upon it. Then, one day, anticipating it and enjoying it are no longer possible, at least not this side of heaven. That feels unnatural…it hurts…and it can go on hurting for a long, long time.

But in our hurting, it's important for us to look up and realize that we are perpetually on God's mind, because He cares for us:

> Just as a father has compassion on his children,
> So the LORD has compassion on those who
>   fear Him.
> For He Himself knows our frame;
> He is mindful that we are but dust…
> But the lovingkindness of the LORD is
>   from everlasting to everlasting on those
>   who fear Him…(Psalm 103:13-14,17).

In caring for us, He helps us, especially through the ministry of the Holy Spirit, the divine Comforter, in our lives:

> The Spirit also helps our weakness; for we do not know
> how to pray as we should, but the Spirit Himself intercedes for us with groanings too deep for words; and He
> who searches the hearts knows what the mind of the
> Spirit is, because He intercedes for the saints according
> to the will of God (Romans 8:26-28).

So, right now—at this very moment, in your precise circumstances, horrible as they may be—pause and consider this: *God is thinking of you.*

You're with Him in His mind.

You matter far more to Him than the stars.

He will be your strength.

From Glenda…Our Times

A time to keep…

ECCLESIASTES 3:6

When you raise a child, he or she is always on your mind.

When your child dies, he or she is always on your mind.

On a day that was especially dark emotionally, Nathan was on my mind. If you are grieving, you know well that, on many days, nothing you see, think, or hear sounds very good. In fact, the darkness can seem endless.

As I've learned to do at such times, I read my Bible—or at least tried to—groping for some ray of light. As I did, my eyes fell on this verse:

> Show me a sign for good,
> That those who hate me may see it and
> be ashamed,
> Because You, O LORD, have helped me
> and comforted me (Psalm 86:17).

That particular day, this verse struck me as medicine to my soul. I have learned the power of praying Scripture in my life, so I immediately prayed, "God, show me a sign for good today."

I believe God led me to that verse then and, in His mercy, He answered my prayer. Around three o' clock that afternoon the doorbell rang, and the UPS man handed me a large envelope with a return address printed in bold navy blue letters. It was from camp—Nathan's place of employment at the time of his death.

At first, my heart sank. The envelope felt as though it contained a letter. I could not help but wonder whether it was a letter Nathan had sent to us before he died, or a poem he had written and someone had found, or a note from someone he knew who just wanted tell us what he had come to mean to them.

I was almost afraid to open it because, while any of those prospects could have been the case, at that moment they would have intensified the tremendous sadness I was already feeling in my heart. Slowly, however, I opened the large envelope and pulled out a note that read: "I thought that you would like to see these letters from our students to Nathan. This group was one of Nathan's last teaching shifts." It was signed by the camp director.

I began to read ten brightly decorated thank-you notes that some of Nathan's last students had written to him. One by one, I treasured and drank in every word of appreciation and hand-drawn decoration on each letter. It was a precious moment because, even in just the brief encounter that Nathan had with these students, they had captured the essence of who he was.

Some of their comments included:

- "Thank you for making science fun."
- "Thank you for funny jokes."
- "Thank you for making me comfortable with activities that scared me."
- "Thank you for making this the best week of my life."

As these students had learned, Nathan was fun, intelligent, compassionate, and energetic. As they spent some of Nathan's final days and hours on earth with him, these students experienced all of who he was. Because God brought me this sign for good, I forgot the sadness for a moment and appreciated in a fresh way what God had made Nathan to be. I paused and gave thanks to God for the gift of Nathan's life and the blessing he was to our family.

Later that night I noticed something startling about this "gift for good" that God had sent. The date at the top of every page was… January 24, 2006.

It was hard to wrap my mind around it, but those letters were all dated the morning that Nathan fell to his death. Even as he entered heaven, and before anyone else on this earth even knew what had happened, words of praise and appreciation were being expressed for his life. I just had to marvel at the mind and ways of God.

Truly, as Jesus said, "Your Father knows what you need before you ask Him" (Matthew 6:8). I still find comfort to this day in that answer to prayer.

In Psalm 16:7-8, David said:

> I will bless the LORD who has counseled me;
> Indeed, my mind instructs me in the night.
> I have set the Lord continually before me;
> Because He is at my right hand, I will not
>   be shaken.

The Lord blessed me that day with a perfect sign for good. He has repeatedly done so during my walk with Him, and I love Him. I will bless the Lord all the rest of the days I have on this earth, because He alone is the only One who can stand by my side through the bad days as well as the good, so that I am not shaken.

The Lord has you too on His mind, all the time, and He is able to comfort and counsel you when you turn your mind toward Him. Perhaps you need "a sign for good" right now. Call out to God. In His way and time, He will hear you and He will answer you. I am confident of it.

14

In His Eye

YOU NEVER KNOW what you're going to find in a seatback pocket on an airplane.

Not long ago, during the course of writing this book, I was traveling to a ministry engagement. Sticking out of the seatback pocket before me was a book titled *At the Back of the North Wind,* written by George MacDonald. As I glanced through it, I realized that part of the message in this "accidental" find was important to include in this book.

MacDonald was a Christian minister and author from Scotland who died in 1905. His writings influenced numerous literary greats, including C.S. Lewis, J.R.R. Tolkien, G.K. Chesterton, Lewis Carroll, and some say, even Mark Twain. *At the Back of the North Wind* is one of his classics.

One theme addressed in MacDonald's works was the problem of the existence of evil in a world where God is sovereign. Some believe he may have based the central character of *At the Back of the North Wind*—a young boy named Diamond—on his own son

Maurice, who died in his teens. (Once again, I was intrigued to discover the real-life tragedy that lies behind some of the most enduring literature.)

In this children's novel, Diamond befriends the North Wind—portrayed as Lady—and then rides on her back through multiple adventures. Diamond is always trying to help others, but in the end he dies. In one interpreter's view, as the story unfolds, "North Wind seems to be a representation of Pain and Death working according to God's will for something good."[1]

At one point near the end of the book, MacDonald narrates a conversation between Diamond and North Wind that helps underscore the wondrous truth that, in our times of grief as well as at all other times, God has His eye upon us.

In the dialogue, North Wind questions Diamond, who is afraid that his friend North Wind is not real but only a dream, and may go away. North Wind then attempts to reassure Diamond.

> "Do you remember what the song you were singing a week ago says about Bo-Peep—how she lost her sheep, but got twice as many lambs?"
>
> "Oh yes, I do, well enough," answered Diamond; "but I never just quite liked that rhyme."
>
> "Why not, child?"
>
> "Because it seems to say that one's as good as another, or two new ones are better than one that's lost. I've been thinking about it a great deal, and it seems to me that although any one sixpence is as good as any other sixpence, not twenty lambs would do instead of one sheep whose face you knew. Somehow, when once you've looked into anybody's eyes, right deep down into them, I mean, nobody will do for that one anymore.

Nobody, ever so beautiful or so good, will make up for that one going out of sight."

Did you catch that last part?

"...not twenty lambs would do instead of one sheep whose face you knew. Somehow, when once you've looked into anybody's eyes, right deep down into them, I mean, nobody will do for that one anymore. Nobody, ever so beautiful or so good, will make up for that one going out of sight."

Probably by now, you've realized the truth of these words in relation to the loved one you're grieving—we certainly have. In this world, *nobody, ever so beautiful or so good, will make up for that one going out of sight.*

This passage brought to mind the painful lack of understanding someone expressed to a friend of ours whose teenage daughter had just died—"At least you're still young enough to have another one," the person said.

It also reminded me that our God ever has us in His eye.

Jesus Himself said, "Are not two sparrows sold for a cent? And yet not one of them will fall to the ground apart from your Father. But the very hairs of your head are all numbered. So do not fear; you are more valuable than many sparrows" (Matthew 10:29-31).

In the Old Testament, Abraham's servant Hagar experienced this truth for herself. Abraham and his wife, Sarah (they were then known as Abram and Sarai), were childless, despite the fact that God had promised the aged Abraham an heir. Taking matters into their own hands:

Abram's wife Sarai took Hagar the Egyptian, her maid, and gave her to her husband Abram as his wife. He

went in to Hagar, and she conceived; and when she
saw that she had conceived, her mistress was despised
in her sight.

Subsequently, "Sarai treated her harshly, and she fled from her presence" (Genesis 16:4-6). In the wilderness where Hagar fled, the angel of the Lord appeared to her, conveying God's promise that He would greatly multiply her descendants so there would be too many to count (verse 10).

Then, I love what Scripture says next: "She called the name of the LORD who spoke to her, 'You are a God who sees'" (Genesis 16:13).

A God who sees—that's how Hagar described the Lord. While God eventually gave Abraham and Sarah the son He had promised them—Isaac—His gracious revelation of Himself to Hagar as "a God who sees" can be of great comfort and encouragement to us in our grief.

One of the difficult aspects of grief lies in the feeling that no one else sees our pain. Even when that is true humanly speaking, it could not be farther from the truth with God.

One day Jesus came upon a funeral procession in which "a dead man was being carried out, the only son of his mother, and she was a widow; and a sizeable crowd from the city was with her."

Scripture then says, "When the Lord *saw* her, He felt compassion for her, and said to her, 'Do not weep'" (Luke 7:12-13).

On this occasion, the Lord performed a miracle and raised the young man from the dead. The fact is that the Son of God *saw* the sorrow of this woman who had lost both her husband and her son and "He felt compassion for her." He does the same for us.

Knowing that we are seen by God Himself is grounds for hope. Though, like David, we may feel that our "eye has wasted away with grief," we can take comfort that "the LORD has heard the voice of my weeping…has heard my supplication…receives my prayer" (Psalm 6:7).

Knowing that "the eye of the LORD is on those…who hope for His lovingkindness" (Psalm 33:18) enables us to say:

> Why are you in despair, O my soul?
> And why have you become disturbed within me?
> Hope in God, for I shall again praise Him
> For the help of His presence (Psalm 42:5).

He is the only One beautiful enough and good enough to "make up for" those who have gone out of our sight.

From Glenda…Our Times

A time to heal…
ECCLESIASTES 3:3

Grief often leads you from pain to action.

You want to move from doing unnecessary tasks into doing what is truly necessary. You want to change anything that is superficial about your life into that which is intentional and meaningful. It has had those effects on us, at least.

We've also found that we want the loss of our son to have an impact for Christ on the lives of others. This has meant that we've spent hours asking God to bring many people to faith in Christ through Nathan's death.

The first characteristic we all valued about Nathan when he died was his courageous heart for God. In thinking about how we could honor Nathan and point people to the One he had followed, we felt led to have any donations in his memory made to a program of the Billy Graham Evangelistic Association called "Dare to Be a Daniel." This program teaches "tweens"—youth between the ages of 9 and 14—to share their faith in Christ, and encourages them in their walk with Him. Nathan's sister JesseRuth, who turned 12 about 3 weeks after he died—benefitted from taking part in the program. We knew that Nathan would be "all about" this plan, so we were thrilled to do it.

The summer before he died, Nathan had run the San Diego marathon. When a group of friends heard about the plan to support "Dare to Be a Daniel," they decided to raise money by getting people to sponsor them in running the next year's San Diego marathon. They called themselves "Team N8"—"N8" was an abbreviation for Nathan's nickname "Nate." We rejoiced that, ultimately, thousands of dollars came in to help young people know and share Christ. Nathan would have been amazed, humbled, and honored to know that his life would add to the number of people who will join him in heaven.

Our whole family went to San Diego to watch "TEAM N8" run the marathon—Gregory and Preston ran in it, while the rest of us cheered. Seeing in person the exact race that Nathan had run the year before was like being in a dream. I vividly remembered talking to him by phone to wish him luck before the race, and then talking to him just after he crossed the finish line to congratulate him.

I was grateful that God allowed me to see firsthand what I had not been able to witness the year before with my sweet son. It made me keenly aware of how hard it is to complete a marathon and what work it takes even to attempt to run one. I am so proud that he set the pace for all of us to challenge ourselves and push our limits, that day and with the rest of our lives.

If you have lost a loved one, right about now you may be saying, "So what?" At this point, you may not care even to think about trying to accomplish anything good with the terrible situation in your life. However, I urge you to consider the fact that God may want to use your horrible circumstance to encourage someone else in their faith, or to bring people you don't even know to Christ.

I would have never expected that Nathan's life—and death—would be used by God to support such a significant ministry. Nor would I have expected to hear from so many people I did not previously know, about how Nathan's walk with the Lord has encouraged them. That's what has happened, however, which brings to mind this Scripture:

> Things which eye has not seen and ear has not heard,
> and which have not entered the heart of man, all that
> God has prepared for those who love him (1 Corinthians
> 2:9).

None of us knows all that God has planned for our lives and for those we love. I have learned that, if we trust and love God, we have to take everything that comes into our lives as being from Him. It is hard to get to the place in some circumstances where we are happy about everything, but we can trust that He will walk with us through it and use it for good.

My eyes saw a son grow into a man of God. There's no way my eyes would have ever been able to see what his future held—but God knew it from before the day he was conceived.

I rest in that fact. I hope it encourages you to do the same with the lives of those who are dear to you.

15

In His Ear

Monday, April 16, 2007. Shortly after seven o'clock that morning, a lone gunman on the campus of Virginia Tech launched a shooting spree that, in a matter of hours, left 32 people dead and numerous others wounded. He then killed himself.

This horrific incident was of course followed by an intensive investigation in an effort to understand how and why it happened. Among the details that emerged, numerous media outlets reported on one particularly haunting aspect of the day's events: *As first responders reached the bodies of slain victims, they heard victims' cell phones ringing with calls from panicked loved ones who were trying to get word of their safety.*

One writer commented:

> As the police cleared the bodies from the Virginia Tech engineering building, the cell phones rang, in the eccentric varieties of ring tones, as parents kept trying to see if their children were O.K. To imagine the feelings of the police as they carried the bodies and heard the

ringing is heartrending; to imagine the feelings of the parents who were calling—dread, desperate hope for a sudden answer and the bliss of reassurance, dawning grief—is unbearable.[1]

Some 15 months before the Virginia Tech shootings, we ourselves experienced that "dread"…that "desperate hope for a sudden answer and the bliss of reassurance"…and then finally that "dawning grief"…as we and others sought to locate Nathan after he did not report for work.

Nathan did not die at the hand of a murderer. We know parents whose children have. Loved ones of those who have done so—whether in the Virginia Tech shooting or in some other act of violence elsewhere—walk through grief that is intensified and complicated by this element.

However, we do know about the frantic calls that go unanswered…the mounting concern that culminates in the realization of our worst fears…and then—through the technology of voice mail—the painful replay of the entire sequence of events. You see, among the personal possessions recovered from the remote area where Nathan's climb began—and ended—was his cell phone.

When I was able to bring myself to check it, 17 unheard messages were waiting. From start to finish, they chronicled the time between when his absence was noticed, and when (and even after) his body was found. These four are from his camp supervisor:

"Hey, Nathan…where are you, man? You're late for your shift!"

"Nathan, give us a call! We're wondering where you are."

"Nathan, we're getting worried about you…give us a call!"

"Nathan, deputies are searching for you…let us know where you are."

At that point, word of Nathan's disappearance had begun to spread, and others—friends, various family members—began to call him.

I listened to those messages, and then came to some that were already quite familiar: they were the messages—ever growing in intensity—that Glenda and I had left him between the time we learned he was missing and when we received notification of his death. Those messages moved from words of concerned inquiry to increasingly fervent pleading for some contact from him that would never come.

Then, the messages on Nathan's phone changed. Even after his body was found, several more still came. They were stunned…tearful…brokenhearted. Of those 17 messages, Nathan didn't hear even one of them.

Maybe at this very moment, in the wake of your own personal loss, you're feeling stunned…tearful…brokenhearted. Maybe you're wondering whether anyone can hear your "message"—that guttural cry of sorrow welling up in your heart.

I'm here to tell you: the answer is *yes!*

Though our son, and perhaps your loved one, didn't answer those last calls, the Bible makes it clear that the living God attunes His ear to those who cry out in faith to Him. This was David's experience. He wrote:

> The eyes of the Lord are toward the righteous
> And His ears are open to their cry…
> The righteous cry, and the Lord hears…
> The Lord is near to the brokenhearted
> And saves those who are crushed in spirit
>   (Psalm 34:15-18).

He also said:

> Hear my cry, O God;
> Give heed to my prayer.
> From the end of the earth I call to You when
>   my heart is faint;
> Lead me to the rock that is higher than I.
> For You have been a refuge for me...
>   (Psalm 61:1-3).

He declared:

> O You who hear prayer,
> To You all men come (Psalm 65:2).

Repeatedly in life, and especially in our grief, I have given thanks that God does indeed "hear prayer." He is the one true God, unlike the gods I've seen as I've traveled to other countries (and even in our own).

On those occasions, I've observed people who are not followers of Christ chanting in temples and bowing at altars to their various gods. I've watched them meticulously adorn stone statues with flowers and light candles and place money before them in an effort to appease them. (I've even seen them worship snakes—not me!)

I've always found it saddening that, in their spiritual blindness, people stoop to devote themselves to human creations like those described by the psalmist:

> Their idols are silver and gold,
> The work of man's hands.
> They have mouths, but they cannot speak;
> They have eyes, but they cannot see;

> They have ears, but they cannot hear;
> They have noses, but they cannot smell;
> They have hands, but they cannot feel;
> They have feet, but they cannot walk;
> They cannot make a sound with their throat
> (Psalm 115:4-7).

However, while their gods are lifeless and impotent, our God is the Almighty One who "became flesh, and dwelt among us" in the person of His Son, the Lord Jesus Christ (John 1:14). He is the One who, by His mighty power, raised Christ from the dead. He is the One who cares for us.

This God has heard and answered our prayers time and time again. He has comforted us, strengthened us, instructed us, and blessed us. Even in our sorrow, we have experienced His mercy, wisdom, and faithfulness.

That's why we can say:

> Blessed be God,
> Who has not turned away my prayer
> Nor His lovingkindness from me
> (Psalm 66:20).

So…in your grief, go ahead and call out to Him, trusting in His Son who is at this moment "within the veil," interceding for us.

Pour out your heart to Him—no night is too dark, and no need is too great. Your prayer will reach His ear. He will hear you, and—in His perfect way and time—He will answer you.

He has done that for us—He will do it for you.

From Glenda…Our Times

He has made everything appropriate in its time…
ECCLESIASTES 3:11

The morning was going fairly well.

It was about a month after Nathan's death, and I had actually been able to accomplish a few menial tasks that I had not attempted in some time.

I answered the phone when it rang, and one of my very best friends began telling me of an encounter that she had with a back-door neighbor who had lived behind us as Nathan was growing up.

My friend said, "Glenda, she told me that she can still hear you calling Nathan's name from your back door, telling him to come home."

At that moment, time stood still. As we grieve, it's not uncommon for a memory to bring whatever is happening around us screeching to a halt and, then, just sit there for us to ponder, wrestle with, laugh about, cry over…or perhaps respond to in all of those ways.

In my mind, I immediately went back to one of the many times when Nathan heard my voice and came running home after playing a fierce game of soccer with his neighborhood friends. The memory both soothed and hurt.

Nathan would come when I called him because he knew my voice—he knew my voice because I am his mother. I knew—and loved—his voice because he was my son.

In fact, I loved his voice so much that, after he died, I could not bring myself to cancel his cell phone for nearly two years. Every so often, I would call it just to listen to his voice: "Hey, this is Nathan. Leave a message and I'll call you back."

When that message would play, I knew without a doubt that the voice was my son's. As his mother, I had listened to that voice from the time he made his first sounds.

The first time I heard his voice after he died, I was wracked with pain. Immediately, though, it was as if God said to me, "Glenda, do you know *My* voice?"

God in His great mercy drew me back to the focal point of my life—Him. In the same way that I know Nathan's voice when I hear it, I know God's voice when I hear it, because of years of spending time praying and listening to Him. I have never heard His voice audibly, but I know when He speaks to me because I have a relationship with Him. And it is His voice that will give me direction and strength through my remaining days on this earth.

In Isaiah 30:21, God promised His people:

> Your ears will hear a word behind you,
> "This is the way, walk in it,"
> whenever you turn to the right or to the left.

One of the things that sorrow has refined in me is the motivation to do what is important to God and to leave behind the superficial or unimportant. I need, and have prayed, to hear His voice behind me at every turn in the road of life saying, "Glenda, this is the way, walk in it."

You can make this your prayer as well. The way to know His voice is to spend time with Him, thinking on His Word and listening for Him to communicate with you. I don't mean you always have to sit idly in a chair waiting to hear from God. As you go about your day, just turn everything over to Him and ask Him to guide you. My day goes something like this:

> "Lord, as I get out of this bed, may my feet walk down your path."

> "Lord, as I read your Word, speak to me."

> "Lord, as I drive JesseRuth to school today, bless her and place her with the people you want her to be with."

> "Lord, as I speak to this person, would you please shine through me."

You get my drift. This has been my practice for as long as I can remember, and it has helped me recognize God's voice when He speaks back to me.

As you read this book, where are you on life's road? Are you at a pivotal moment? Do you need direction? Do you need to hear His voice say, "This is the way, walk in it"?

God's voice is more powerful than any other voice that may clamor for our attention, and His voice endures forever. It gives me hope. It's worth getting to know.

16

In His Hand

ONE SUNDAY MORNING, while a pastor was preaching to his congregation, a man began walking down the center aisle of the church sanctuary.

In some churches this isn't an unusual occurrence—people come forward and kneel for prayer whenever they feel moved to do so, and then return quietly to their seats. There was nothing quiet about this man, however. As he strode down the aisle, he began announcing to the crowd in a loud voice, "I am Christ! I am Christ!"

The church was a large one, and the stunned congregation was staring, wondering what would happen next. To say the least, the pastor had a situation on his hands. What was he to do?

In a moment of inspiration that could only have come from heaven—and as the man continued making a spectacle by repeating, "I am Christ! I am Christ!—the pastor interrupted him and said, somewhat quietly, "Show me your hands."

"What?" the somewhat startled man stopped and asked. "What did you say?"

This time, the pastor said it louder.

"Show me your hands!"

Pausing for a moment, the man slowly reflected on the pastor's challenge, glanced at his hands, and then held them up for the pastor to see.

"Just as I thought!" the pastor declared. "You, sir, are an imposter."

"How do you know?" the man asked.

"Because," said the pastor, firmly, "the prints of the nails are missing. You are not Jesus Christ. His hands were marked by the nails that held Him to the cross."

With that pronouncement, the imposter had been debunked and the incident was over. Of course, the man was a fraud for plenty of other reasons as well. However, this encounter reminds us of an important truth: *As we walk through times of grief, we can find hope in knowing that the loving hand of God—a hand literally marked through Christ's excruciating sacrifice for us on the cross—steadfastly holds us.*

Centuries before Christ appeared, the prophet Isaiah said:

> Behold, the LORD's hand is not so short
> That it cannot save;
> Nor is His ear so dull
> That it cannot hear (Isaiah 59:1).

He also said:

> Can a woman forget her nursing child
> And have no compassion on the son of her womb?
> Even these may forget, but I will not forget you.
> Behold, I have inscribed you on the palms of
>   My hands…(Isaiah 49:15-16).

In the Bible, references to God's hands often picture His power. Realizing that God's all-powerful hands hold us, especially during our greatest times of weakness and vulnerability, gives us comfort and strength. The apostle Thomas, who initially doubted the Lord's resurrection, discovered this for himself, as he encountered quite literally the nail-marked hand of the risen Lord.

On the day Christ rose from the grave, He appeared to some of His disciples. The Scripture says:

> Thomas, one of the twelve, called Didymus, was not with them when Jesus came. So the other disciples were saying to him, "We have seen the Lord!"
>
> But he said to them, "Unless I see in His hands the imprint of the nails, and put my finger into the place of the nails, and put my hand into His side, I will not believe."
>
> After eight days His disciples were again inside, and Thomas with them. Jesus came, the doors having been shut, and stood in their midst and said, "Peace be with you."
>
> Then He said to Thomas, "Reach here with your finger, and see My hands; and reach here your hand and put it into My side; and do not be unbelieving, but believing."
>
> Thomas answered and said to Him, "My Lord and my God!" (John 20:24-28).

Thomas saw the marks of the nails in the hands of Jesus, and what he saw caused his doubts to flee. Jesus went on to tell him, "Because you have seen Me, have you believed? Blessed are they who did not see, and yet believed" (John 20:29). Even though we have not

seen Him as Thomas did, we need not doubt either the Lord's resurrection victory or His care for us.

The psalmist said:

> He is our God,
> And we are the people of His pasture, and
> the sheep of His hand (Psalm 95:6-7).

Jesus spoke of those who trust in Him as being like sheep in His
hand, saying:

> My sheep hear My voice, and I know them, and they
> follow Me; and I give eternal life to them, and they will
> never perish; and no one will snatch them out of My
> hand. My Father, who has given them to Me, is greater
> than all; and no one is able to snatch them out of the
> Father's hand (John 10:27-29).

During the course of His earthly ministry, Christ frequently
reached out His hand and touched people, including those that society deemed untouchable. In our grief—and always—we are in His
hand, and that's important for us to know.

Some people aren't particularly "touch" people (and some who
are "touch" people overdo it with others who aren't!). Perhaps,
though, you have experienced, as we have, that just having a family member, friend, or pastor simply place a loving hand on your
shoulder can communicate beyond words that you are not isolated
or cut off in your grief.[1]

At times, a caring human hand has made all the difference as we
have sorrowed. We'll be forever grateful for the many people who
have reached out to us, both literally and in various practical ways.

How much more it helps to realize with the psalmist that, no matter how difficult our experience may be:

> You have enclosed me behind and before,
> And laid Your hand upon me (Psalm 139:5).

This day, hear this truth, and cherish it in your heart: *God Himself holds you in His hand.*

In your grief, know that His almighty, loving hand will continually infuse you with the power you need for each day of this journey.

From Glenda…Our Times

A time for peace…
Ecclesiastes 3:8

The first time I held Nathan after his birth, one of the features I noticed about him was his hands. They were tiny, yet strong. We all have characteristics that mark who we are, and Nathan's hands were definitely one of the notable things that marked him.

When he was a toddler he was active, and his hands could move at lightning speed to reach for something he wasn't supposed to have or to perform some act of mischief. As he grew into a man, it was his hands that so often enabled him to perform the activities and tasks he loved: climbing mountain rock faces, tying every kind of knot imaginable and setting up ropes courses, demonstrating science facts at camp, writing poetry and songs, playing the guitar, and even crocheting.

Nathan was always doing something with his hands, and I am still coming across things he created. Every now and then, I'll open a drawer and find a random piece of paper on which he wrote his thoughts or a beaded necklace he made. The other day I was looking for something warm to wear in the snow and came across the toboggan he crocheted for me just weeks before he died. In fact, that year he made a stocking cap for every member of our family.

Memories of holding my child's hand in my own have pointed me to what may be the greatest lesson I have learned in these days of grief—namely, that my heavenly Father wants me to put my own hand into His and let Him hold me.

Grief often makes you feel like a little child who is lost. I know it sounds silly, and I am not proud to admit it, but it is true. I have had to say, "Lord, I feel lost and I am going to put my hand in yours. Will You lead me?" His hand has indeed led me.

Recently, I spent some time in the Scriptures studying the significance of God's hand. One passage in particular caught my attention. It includes this statement: "The hand of the LORD was on Elijah, and he girded up his loins and outran Ahab to Jezreel" (1 Kings 18:46).

In this passage, Elijah had just seen God demonstrate His power in an amazing way. In a confrontation with 450 prophets of the idol Baal, he had called on the name of the Lord, and God responded by sending fire from heaven. Elijah then slew the idolatrous prophets. Afterward, in response to Elijah's prayer, God sent rain to relieve the drought gripping the land. God then gave Elijah the supernatural ability to run faster than King Ahab's horse-drawn chariot some 17 miles.

These events angered Jezebel, the wife of King Ahab, and she sought to kill Elijah. This made the battle-weary Elijah feel lonely and afraid. But once again, God placed His hand on Elijah and strengthened him. By an angel, He delivered to him some food that energized and sustained him for the next 40 days.

Maybe right now you're feeling somewhat like Elijah—exhausted, weaker than you have felt ever before in your life. Maybe you just want to quit, to lie down and die. If so, like Elijah, now is the time for you to call out to God. As you do, you'll experience that He strengthens us with His hand.

Isaiah 41:10 says:

> Do not fear, for I am with you;
> Do not anxiously look about you, for I am
>   your God.
> I will strengthen you, surely I will help you,
> Surely I will uphold you with My righteous
>   right hand."

Psalm 136:12 speaks of God helping His people with "a strong hand and an outstretched arm." Why? Because "His lovingkindness is everlasting."

Personally, I know this to be true. There were many days right after Nathan's death in which I did not know how I was going to make it through the next few hours. I would call out to Jesus and ask Him to help me. He was always faithful to answer that prayer. I got through each of those days, and He is still helping me get through each day, though it is generally not as difficult now. His hand is strong and embraces us in our pain.

Of course, I miss receiving fresh demonstrations of Nathan's handiwork, which meant so much not only to us but also to others. One recent Christmas we received a message from Nathan's camp director, Allan. He said, "We always remember Nathan around

Christmastime because of the Christmas placemats Nathan made for us, which are such a great example of Nathan's quirky but so very genuine way of showing love."

God's handiwork, however, is newly visible every day. When we miss holding the hand of someone we have loved, God's hand is always there to hold us until we meet Him face-to-face. He will strongly support us when we call upon Him.

17

In His Heart

I'VE SEEN THEM countless times.

Probably you've noticed them too, maybe paying more attention to them now because of your own experience.

You may even have one.

What I'm referring to are the cars and trucks I see on the road, on which the rear windows bear decals or lettering expressing remembrance of a person who has died. Typically, the messages include the deceased person's name, the years of his or her birth and death, and a sentiment such as:

> "In loving memory of…"
>
> "Gone but not forgotten…"
>
> "In our hearts forever…"

Although I've seen them many times, only after Nathan died did all that they represent begin to register with me. Each such message has behind it a story…a story of both joy and pain…a story that quite literally goes with its bearers everywhere, all the time.

Recently, for example, I saw a car that bore the name of an infant boy who lived just six weeks. Having had four children and now several grandchildren—and having buried a son—that message did more than just briefly register with me.

My first reaction was that, in a society that often demeans the value of preborn and newborn life, I appreciated the recognition and dignity those parents were affording to that little one.

Then I looked at the young couple in the car and began to think of all that they must have been through (and must still be going through) with the death of their child—

- whom they had lovingly conceived together…
- whose impending arrival they learned of with both nervousness and celebration…
- whose birth they anticipated and prepared for…
- whose appearance they no doubt marveled at…
- whose first days outside the mother's womb involved for them both rejoicing and sleep deprivation…
- whose lifeless body they looked upon with stunned disbelief, and perhaps wailing…
- whose funeral they had to plan, and endure…
- and then, whose too-soon departure they have mourned and agonized over, and struggled to live beyond ever since.

Just thinking through their probable story brings tears to my eyes.

Maybe some people would scoff that I'm merely imagining, and perhaps even exaggerating, their plight. I didn't know them, so maybe I am. However, I guarantee you that just such a scenario holds true for others—perhaps you.

We carry those we love in our hearts for all our days. However, whatever affection we have in our hearts is a mere token of that which resides in God, who is love (1 John 4:8). In our grief, we can find comfort in knowing that we are ever in His heart.

The Old Testament gives us a striking picture of this truth. In the book of Exodus, God was giving instructions for how Israel was to worship Him. As part of those instructions, He specified the garments that Moses' brother Aaron, the high priest, was to wear. He said:

> You shall make a breastpiece of judgment…You shall mount on it four rows of stones; the first row shall be a row of ruby, topaz and emerald; and the second row a turquoise, a sapphire and a diamond; and the third row a jacinth, an agate and an amethyst; and the fourth row a beryl and an onyx and a jasper; they shall be set in gold filigree (Exodus 28:15,17-20).

How stunning all those jewels set in gold on Aaron's garment must have been! But notice their significance:

> The stones shall be according to the names of the sons of Israel: twelve, according to their names; they shall be like the engravings of a seal, each according to his name for the twelve tribes (verse 21).

What was Aaron to do with these jewels bearing the names of the tribes of Israel?

> Aaron shall carry the names of the sons of Israel in the breastpiece of judgment over his heart when he enters the holy place, for a memorial before the LORD continually…They shall be over Aaron's heart when he goes in before the LORD; and Aaron shall carry the judgment of the sons of Israel over his heart before the LORD continually (verses 29-30).

Think of it—God decreed that the one person on the face of the earth authorized to appear before Him in the holiest chamber of His tabernacle was to bear on his heart jewels named for His people. How much more does our Great High Priest, the Lord Jesus Christ, bear us in His heart as He intercedes for us "within the veil."

What depth this truth imparts to our worship now. Glenda and I have commented often that, for us, times of worshipping the Lord are also the times we find ourselves feeling closest to Nathan. The reason is that, while we cannot communicate with Nathan, we *can* worship God with him. He just happens to have a much better seat!

Nathan's camp director made a similar point in a note he sent us a couple of years after Nathan's death. He wrote:

> We loved Nathan and look forward to worshipping The GREAT I AM together with him in the not-so-distant future. We are lifted by the thought that at all moments Nathan is doing just that in the fulfilling limitlessness of heaven, no longer fettered by the things we watched him struggle with so valiantly during the time he was with us. He will always be our little lion-heart.

Yes…amen…and we are always in God's heart. Hallelujah!

From Glenda…Our Times

He has also set eternity in their heart…
ECCLESIASTES 3:11

The UPS truck pulled into our driveway as I was standing outside talking with a friend.

I became distracted as he unloaded some boxes.

These were the boxes that contained Nathan's earthly belongings. We had packed them weeks earlier in California. I was in such a fog then that I could not even remember what was in them. For days and weeks after they arrived at our home, the boxes remained unopened.

One night, as I could not sleep, I made my way in the dark downstairs to Preston's study. There, the boxes sat quietly, yet "speaking"— speaking of Nathan and beckoning to be opened. I decided to use these moments alone to open them. I was thinking that doing so might ease the pain I was feeling in my heart from missing my son.

I had barely cracked open the first box when a familiar aroma reached my nose. It smelled just like Nathan. He loved to wear patchouli, derived from a plant that emits a pungent fragrance and that some use as an insect repellant. Everything he touched and owned smelled like it. I really didn't like the smell and often told him so. However, in the stillness and darkness of that moment, I inhaled deeply like a person gasping for air.

I opened one box and then, feverishly, another. At times, I would hold his clothes up to my face and breath in, sobbing all the while. I have no idea how long I lingered over those boxes in those early morning hours, but I know it was a long time. By the time I was finished, the entire room smelled like…NATHAN.

It was a moment in which I felt a connection to Nathan. At the same time, though, it felt so empty because he was not there and all I had to hold were these few possessions from his time on this earth. In my emptiness and pain, I wanted desperately to call out to Nathan. I may have even done that, but there was no response, nor could there be.

However, I did call out to Jesus, who comforted and helped me so that, after some time, I could go back to bed. Over the next days, I reflected on this event. As I did so, God seemed to ask me a very important question, "Glenda is *your* life a fragrant aroma?"

The Bible says, "Walk in love, just as Christ also loved you and gave Himself up for us, an offering and a sacrifice to God as a fragrant aroma" (Ephesians 5:2).

Christ's life on this earth—and above all, His sacrifice on the cross for our sins—was "a fragrant aroma" to His Father. It also left a sweet fragrance for us to immerse ourselves in for eternity. As I thought about this truth, I realized that, if I am in a relationship with Him and growing to be more and more like Him, then even in my pain my life too should be a fragrant aroma, both to God and to others.

The apostle Paul said, "We are a fragrance of Christ to God among those who are being saved and among those who are perishing; to the one an aroma from death to death, to the other an aroma from life to life And who is adequate for these things?" (2 Corinthians 2:15-16).

I have had to come to terms with the fact that my life is ultimately not mine to plan for myself. God laid out a plan for me, a purpose for my existence, long ago, even before I was born. Because He has done so, I can embrace all this pain and sorrow knowing that He already knows about it and will walk with me through it. He will produce in and through me the fragrant aroma that He wants my life to have. He will use all that befalls me to glorify Himself. Many times, I don't know how—or honestly, why—but I can trust Him to do it.

Perhaps all that these days have held for us will help someone else who is walking through the death of a loved one. Maybe that someone else is you. If so, then I will give Him the thanks and the praise.

God placed on my heart the idea for this book about six months after Nathan died. I just sensed that, in all the pain and suffering, He was teaching me much about who He is. I knew that I was to write it down. In His great mercy, He has brought me closer to Him, and He longs to do the same for you. We are praying that, in the days to come, God will comfort you and that you will experience His presence—and find His hope—as you never have before.

In this world, death will continue to be part of our human experience. The reality of this life is that, one day, we will all step into eternity, either to live forever in the presence of God or to dwell forever separated from Him in a place the Bible calls hell. Christ, though, is our hope. Through a relationship with Him, we can live with Him in heaven in a fullness that no man can grasp.

There, we will celebrate that He *is* the fragrant aroma of our lives.

Conclusion

THE LAST TIME I saw Nathan alive was at the Charlotte airport. His Christmas break had drawn to a close, and it was time for him to return to camp in California. He loved investing in the kids there, and savored living in one of America's prime rock-climbing areas.

As we drove to the airport, it was early in the morning—still dark. At that hour, we didn't talk a lot. En route, however, I made a point of breaking the predawn quiet to say:

"Nathan, I love you."

"I love you, Dad," he replied.

Within just a few minutes, we were approaching the terminal. We drove up the ramp to the departure level and rolled to a stop in front of a door. He got out of the car on his side. I got out on mine, and helped him get his arms around his bag of gear and the assorted other rolled-up-tied-up possessions he had accumulated during Christmas.

Once he was loaded down—amid the surrounding stops and starts of other vehicles discharging passengers for far-flung destinations—I gave him a quick hug, glanced for an instant at his face, and watched for a moment as he trekked into the terminal. Then I got back into the car and drove off.

That was it.

The next time I saw "him"—a little more than three weeks later—was also early morning, but it was at our church. Our funeral director was, with his staff, carefully removing from the back of a hearse the casket bearing Nathan's body.

What lay in that casket wasn't really Nathan—it was just the emptied, lifeless tent that he had left behind. The real Nathan—a redeemed soul, saved through faith in Jesus Christ—was now in heaven with the Lord he loved.

Since then it has occurred to me that last seeing him at an airport was appropriate. After all, the next time I see him may well be in the air.

That's what the Bible teaches. Before His death, Jesus told His disciples: "You too have grief now; but I will see you again, and your heart will rejoice, and no one will take your joy away from you" (John 16:22).

After Jesus rose from the grave, He met with His disciples in Galilee.

> He was lifted up while they were looking on, and a cloud received Him out of their sight. And as they were gazing intently into the sky while He was going, behold, two men in white clothing stood beside them. They also said, "Men of Galilee, why do you stand looking into the sky? This Jesus, who has been taken up from you into heaven, will come in just the same way as you have watched Him go into heaven" (Acts 1:9-11).

As those angels declared, Christ's ascension to heaven was far from being the last time anyone will see Him. The apostle Paul wrote:

> This we say to you by the word of the Lord, that we who are alive and remain until the coming of the Lord, will not precede those who have fallen asleep. For the Lord Himself will descend from heaven with a shout, with the voice of the archangel and with the trumpet of God, and the dead in Christ will rise first. Then we who are alive and remain will be caught up together with them in the clouds to meet the Lord in the air, and so we shall always be with the Lord. Therefore comfort one another with these words (1 Thessalonians 4:15-18).

Paul also urged Christ's followers to be "looking for the blessed hope and the appearing of the glory of our great God and Savior, Christ Jesus" (Titus 2:13).

So…unless the Lord takes me to heaven before He returns for His children, the next time I see Nathan will indeed be in the air. That plot of ground, where at this moment his corpse lies buried, will burst open and give him up for a grand reunion in the sky.

However, as sweet as that reunion will be—with Nathan, and with my father, and with all those who have preceded me into the Lord's presence—the focal point of that moment will be our Redeemer, the Lord Jesus Christ. He alone is our hope, and in Him every other need is met, fulfilled, and satisfied.

The vision given to the apostle John, recorded in the closing pages of Scripture, will indeed eventually come to pass:

> I heard a loud voice from the throne, saying, "Behold,

the tabernacle of God is among men, and He will dwell among them, and they shall be His people, and God Himself will be among them, and He will wipe away every tear from their eyes; and there will no longer be any death; there will no longer be any mourning, or crying, or pain" (Revelation 21:3-4).

One of multiple blessings contained in this promise, I believe, is that even if you are presently living with the anguish of not knowing whether a loved one entered eternity having trusted in Christ for forgiveness and salvation, God will, as you trust Him, "wipe away every tear" and comfort you, as only He can.

Until then, will living with grief continue to be difficult? Yes—more difficult than those who have not yet tasted it full-force for themselves can ever imagine, and in myriad ways.

Job said:

> If a man dies, will he live again?
> All the days of my struggle I will wait
> Until my change comes (Job 14:14).

However, in Christ the struggle has purpose. That purpose is in knowing Him and making Him known, and He doesn't leave us comfortless. Just as surely as He is God and does what He promises, He will not leave us waiting forever. That is certainly "blessed hope"…hope that draws us ever onward.

It's important to keep looking ahead. Paul said, "If we have hoped in Christ in this life only, we are of all men most to be pitied" (1 Corinthians 15:19).

Whatever struggles we are facing now, and whatever challenges may confront each of us in the future, we can find hope in the fact that God Himself knows them…God cares about us…God can carry us safely through them…and God will indeed show Himself faithful and strong in our lives.

We've found that, if we draw near to Him, He draws near to us. What it all comes down to is this:

- Jesus is enough
- Jesus is the only One who is enough
- Jesus is more than enough.

This is our testimony. Our prayer is that it will be your experience too.

"Now may the God of hope fill you with all joy and peace in believing, so that you will abound in hope by the power of the Holy Spirit" (Romans 15:13).

Notes

Chapter 1—Hope: What It Is

1. Portions of this book, including this statement, are excerpted or adapted from Preston Parrish, *Windows into the Heart of God: 31 Life-Changing Glimpses of Jesus* (Eugene, OR: Harvest House, 2007). Later chapters of that book mentioned our family's sorrow, but they did not include many of the experiences and insights that subsequently unfolded and that we now share in this book.

2. Samuel Johnson, *The Rambler*, number 182 (December 14, 1751): www.victorian web.org/previctorian/johnson/rambler182.html.

Chapter 4—The Meaning of Grief

1. C.S. Lewis, *A Grief Observed* (New York: Harper Collins Publishers, 2000), xxi.

2. Ibid., 3, 10, 33, 35, 36.

3. Andrew Miga, "Mom fights to be buried with soldier son," *Dayton Daily News*, December 28, 2009: www.daytondailynews.com/news/nation-world -news/mom fights-to-be-buried-with-soldier-son-467543.html.

Chapter 5—The Magnitude of Grief

1. "September 2001 Disasters." Infoplease: www.infoplease.com/ipa/A0884259 .html.

Part 3—The Certainty: God's Deed and Word

1. Johnson, *The Rambler*, number 203 (February 25, 1752): www.wwnorton
   .com/college/english/nael/noa/pdf/27636_Rest_U11_Johnson.pdf.

Chapter 6—The Resurrection of Christ

1. Here are two helpful books about the evidence for Christ's resurrection: Josh
   McDowell, *Evidence That Demands a Verdict* (Nelson) and Lee Strobel, *The
   Case for Christ and the Case for Faith* (Zondervan). Also, visit Daryl Witmer's
   AIIA Institute at aiia.christiananswers.net.

Chapter 7—The Word of God

1. To read more on the significance of writing letters to others, read Mark
   DeMoss, "Buy Some Stamps" in *The Little Red Book of Wisdom* (Nashville:
   Thomas Nelson, 2007), 36-46.

2. The story of Christ—before He came, while He was here, and since He departed—is the subject of our book *Windows into the Heart of God: 31 Life-
   Changing Glimpses of Jesus* (Eugene, OR: Harvest House, 2007). We wrote
   it to help readers know Him better.

3. Here are three helpful resources on the reliability of the Bible: F.F. Bruce, *The
   Canon of Scripture* (Downer's Grove, IL: InterVarsity Press, 1988); Philip W.
   Comfort, *The Origin of the Bible* (Wheaton, IL: Tyndale House, 2003); and
   James MacDonald, *God Wrote a Book* (Wheaton, IL: Crossway Books, 2004).

Chapter 9—In Every Place

1. Andrew Birkin, *J.M. Barrie and the Lost Boys* (New Haven, CT: Yale Uni-
   versity Press, 2003), 4.

Chapter 10—In Every Outward Circumstance

1. Dietrich Bonhoeffer, *Prisoner for God: Letters and Papers from Prison* (New
   York: Macmillan, 1959), 24.

2. Bonhoeffer, *Prisoner for God*: From the editor's foreword by Eberhard Bethge.

3. "Detrich Bonhoeffer," *Wikipedia*: en.wikipedia.org/wiki/Dietrich_Bonhoeffer
   #cite_note-Eberhard_Bethge_p._927-27.

Chapter 11—In Every Inner Condition

1. Johnson, *The Rambler,* number 67 (November 6, 1750): www.samueljohn
son.com/hope.html#722.

2. "What Is Depression?" *WebMD*; www.webmd.com/depression/guide/what
-is-depression.

3. Anne Barbour, *The Story of Perfect Love* (Billy Graham Evangelistic Association, 2005), available at www.johnandannebarbour.com.

Chapter 14—In His Eye

1. "At the Back of the North Wind," *Wikipedia*: en.wikipedia.org/wiki/At_the
_back_of_the_north_wind.

Chapter 15—In His Ear

1. Adam Gopnik, "Shootings," *New Yorker,* April 30, 2007; www.newyorker
.com/talk/comment/2007/04/30/070430taco_talk_gopnik.

Chapter 16—In His Hand

1. To learn more about communicating care for others, see Gary Chapman,
The 5 Love Languages: The Secret to Love That Lasts (Chicago: Northfield
Publishing, 2010).

Also available by Preston Parrish…

When we draw near to Jesus, amazing things happen. In *Windows into the Heart of God*, you will take a 31-day journey that encourages, builds up, and challenges you to flourish in you personal relationship with the Lord Jesus Christ—a journey that will leave you forever changed!

To learn more about other Harvest House books or to read sample chapters, log on to our website:

www.harvesthousepublishers.com

HARVEST HOUSE PUBLISHERS

EUGENE, OREGON